BreakOUT

UNLEASH THE POWER OF HUMAN CAPITAL

FOR YOURSELF.

FOR THOSE YOU LEAD.

Richard C. Huseman, Ph.D.
Pamela A. Bilbrey

Equity Press

Library of Congress Cataloging-in-Publication Data

PRISM is copyrighted by
Richard C. Huseman, Ph.D.

Relational Intelligence (RQ) is copyrighted by
Richard C. Huseman, Ph.D.

Cover design by Emagination Unlimited, Inc.
www.emaginationunlimited.com

Huseman, Richard C.
Breakout: unleash the power of human capital
Richard C. Huseman, Pamela A. Bilbrey
p.   cm.

ISBN: 0-9712260-5-9
1. Leadership   2. Human Capital   3. Human Thought
4.Human Perception   5. Organizational Change
6. Employee Motivation – United States

Printed in the United States of America

BREAK**OUT**
UNLEASH THE POWER OF HUMAN CAPITAL

FOR YOURSELF.
FOR THOSE YOU LEAD.

RICHARD C. HUSEMAN, PhD   PAMELA A. BILBREY

To learn more about **B**REAK**OUT** and related
workshops, seminars, training programs, leadership
assessment instruments, and quantity discounts for this
plus other publications... or to contact Dick Huseman or
Pam Bilbrey directly, please email
rhuseman@richardchuseman.com or
pbilbrey@bhcpns.org.

NOTES FROM THE AUTHORS

My interest in human capital was sparked during conversations in the late 1990's with a friend and colleague, Jim Seneff. Jim started an ongoing dialogue with me about the value and importance of the employees in all his companies. Jim was interested in how he could best maximize the energy and potential of people. Our conversations resulted in the formation of a Human Capital Committee for Trustreet Properties, a publicly traded company for which I serve as an independent board member. In his role as Chairman of the Board, Jim invited me to chair this committee. As a part of its mission, the Human Capital Committee established a Workplace of Choice committee made up of employees at every level of the organization coming together to create a better organization by making it a "great" place to work.

My work with these committees gave me first hand knowledge and experience that there is a vast untapped reservoir out there of human "talent" or human capital. The more I learned and researched, the more intrigued I became with the potential power of human capital as a means of making huge leaps in terms of both organizational and personal success. The BreakOUT book idea was born.

As I started pulling the ideas for the book together, I became aware of an organization in Pensacola, Florida that had undergone a major BreakOUT – Baptist Health Care. It was there that I met Pam Bilbrey, President of the Baptist Health Care Leadership Institute, for the first time and I realized that I had met someone who had undergone and lived to tell about a massive cultural transition. After getting to know her, I knew she was the perfect person to collaborate on the BreakOUT book with me. The follow pages are the result of this collaboration.

Dick Huseman

Having lived through and witnessed first-hand the major BreakOUT that occurred at Baptist Health Care, I was intrigued by the idea that there might be a set of fundamental principles that could trigger BreakOUT in other organizations. In the years since our BreakOUT at Baptist Health Care, we have literally had thousands of leaders come to Pensacola to hear our story. Dick was one of them. He, in turn, offered a story, as well. He wanted to take his knowledge and experience, couple it with ours at Baptist, and see if there really weren't some real and executable principles that could help any and all organizations achieve the type of BreakOUT that we did at Baptist. Dick asked me to collaborate on the book. I said, "Count me in."

Pam Bilbrey

No book of this nature is the sole product of its authors. The hundreds of leaders and organizations we have interacted with over the years have all in one way or another influenced this final product. We thank them all.

In terms of doing the tedious and painstaking job of proofing the final manuscript, we wish to offer our most sincere thanks to Kathy Edwards for her invaluable assistance. Kathy also contributed by doing initial drafts of some of the BreakOUT practices.

We are especially indebted to Zulema Seguel, who was responsible for overall coordination and made major contributions to the style and content of this project. She, in many ways, pushed both of us to write this book in what we hope is a very readable and engaging way. Thank you, Zu.

And finally, to our families. Their love, support and patience during the development of this book were invaluable.

Dick and Pam

B<small>REAK</small>OUT

Table of Contents

Part I:
BreakOUT: People, Prisons and PCC's

Part II:

BreakOUT: Understanding Human Behavior As Your Key Out of Prison

Chapter 5: The ABC's of Behavior

Chapter 6: Relational Intelligence

Chapter 7: BreakOUT Mapping

Part III:
Creating A Workplace of Choice BreakOUT Human Capital Practices

Chapter 11: BreakOUT Engagement Practices

(How To Get People To Say "I Do") **181**

Chapter 12: BreakOUT Culture Practices

(Cultivating Cultures of Choice) **201**

Epilogue

(The Biggest BreakOUT Of All) **217**

BreakOUT

Prologue

(The Answer To Why)

> Leaders:
>
> *"People are our most valuable asset"*
>
> Everyone Else:
>
> *"Prove It"*

We want to ask you a question. For the most part, do you think people are:

☐ Productive and imaginative

☐ Lazy and dull

What beliefs brought you to your answer? Is it based on a past experience with a person or group of people or did you come to your answer by looking at the human race as a whole? As homo sapiens, we have gone from hiding from predators in caves to sending our greetings out to the stars. We have also caused incomprehensible harm to one another and to our world. The examination of the value of human existence is far beyond the scope of this book or the analysis of its authors.

However, what is important to you, ***as a leader***, is to really know how you actually think about people. Be honest with yourself. It is very easy to say that you value the people you interact with every day but do you actually ***act*** like you do?

Lots of research now proves that it is people who generate value in organizations… not buildings, machines or cash. Yet, despite all the data, many leaders still seem to treat people as pawns in the game. Are you one of these leaders?

The Irony Of The Agony

One of the best cultural icons for the double standard used within Corporate America in terms of how leaders say they value people versus how they actually treat people can be found in the comic strip Dilbert. Scott Adams has made a fortune depicting the many bizarre and counterproductive ways companies and their leaders treat employees.

The humor of Dilbert comes from the irony that Dilbert's sad and tortured existence is in many cases an accurate reflection of what many people face in their every day work environment.

Far too many of us are overworked, underpaid, under-recognized, and undervalued by our leaders. The era of downsizing, merger and acquisition, outsourcing of work (especially overseas) and just plain poor corporate decision-making has made employee loyalty a punishable offense.

The old employment credo:

> *If you work hard and take care of the company,*
> *the company will take care of you*

has become a myth… a story of times long since past. In its place has come a new employee motto:

> *Treat me badly, and I'll get even. I'll give you less work,*
> *sloppier work or I may just not come in again – ever.*
> *And, I may take my skills and talent to your competitor!*

As leaders, we must fully realize that people are the only "real" resource we have. Without them we stand at the cliff's edge alone… or even worse, we stand at the edge with our backs to a bunch of people who couldn't care less whether we fly or fall (in some cases, they wouldn't mind giving us a strong push).

Should we value the people we lead? Common sense says, "Of course, we should!" But again and again and again, and yet again, leaders offer their people the short end of the stick and then pitch the stick off the edge of the cliff.

We all need to watch out. The time of employer as master and employees as servants is long gone… and many leaders have not adjusted to the new era of employee rule.

Employees are increasingly becoming the new masters of the employer-worker relationship and, as such, the standard for strong, effective leadership is going to reach all time heights. Some steps have been made to get the word out before now warning leaders that times are changing and that they need to really put a high premium on the value of people. This next section will provide a brutally brief overview of what research has been done up to now.

The Latest Corporate Lingo – "Human" Capital

Okay! Corporations have started to retool their lingo in regard to the people who work for them. This isn't the first try at this. We started with "employment offices," then "personnel departments," then moved to "human resource departments," and have now, in some organizations, the term has evolved into "human capital" departments. This dispassionate, if not slightly condescending new phrase, has come into use to help those "balance-sheet focused" leaders to really see the value of the organic element in the success equation.

You see, MBA's trained by most major universities have been far better educated to deal with figures than their fellows. In order to plead the case for leadership to be more than planning the best strategy for a big dividend next quarter, proponents of "people-focused" leadership have started to compile data in a way that even the stodgiest of bean counters could appreciate. And they gave their efforts a name that would appeal to the financially familiar: Human Capital. You see, those of the auditing ilk know all about capital.

> **Cap·i·tal /k á p i t' l/**
>
> **1 a :** accumulated wealth **b :** funds, stocks, finance(s); means, property, resources **c :** accumulated possessions calculated to bring in income **d :** net worth

The term "human capital" originates with Theodore Schultz, an economist studying how to best aid developing economies. What Dr. Schultz found was that in order to help the impoverished people of underdeveloped nations, what was needed was knowledge – not land, not machinery and not even energy. Schultz, who won the Nobel Prize in 1979, described this human side of economics as follows:

Consider all human abilities to be either innate or acquired. Every person is born with a particular set of genes, which determines his innate ability. Attributes of acquired population quality, which are valuable and can be augmented by appropriate investment, will be treated as human capital.

A far older and far simpler explanation of human capital can be found if we go back to the time of Chinese Taoist Philosopher, Lao Tze (c. 600 B.C.E.).

If you give a man a fish, you will feed him once.
If you take a man fishing, you will feed him for a week.
If you teach a man to fish, he will never be hungry.

Our unique ability to learn, and from this learned knowledge, to create more knowledge, gives us as humans our true value.

Based on the book, **The ROI of Human Capital** by Jac Fitzenz, we examine the concept of human capital and place it into a business context.

Hu·man Cap·i·tal

1 a : attributes beyond innate ability which are valuable and can be augmented by appropriate investment **b :** traits people bring to a job: intelligence, energy, a generally positive attitude, reliability, commitment **c :** a person's ability to learn: aptitude, imagination, creativity, "street smarts" and savvy

So, we have started to quantify human value as something that might be translatable to a profit-and-loss statement. But now comes the next question, how does human capital impact the bottom line?

Proof In The Pudding

In their book, **The Human Capital Edge**, Bruce Pfau and Ira Kay use a combination of three Watson Wyatt studies to build their argument that human capital management has a clear and positive impact on shareholder value creation. They use something called the HCI (Human Capital Index). What they found was that companies with low HCI scores (i.e., poor human capital management practices) also have low shareholder value creation. As you might expect, they found that companies with high HCI scores (i.e., very effective human capital management practices) also showed high shareholder value creation.

5-Year Total Return to Shareholders

HCI Score	5-Year Total Return To Shareholders	
Low		21%
Medium		39%
High		64%

In case you're curious what "human capital management practices" are, they are a list of several specific corporate practices that are grouped under the general categories of:

- Recruiting and Retention Excellence
- Total Rewards and Accountability
- Collegial, Flexible Workplace

- Communication Integrity
- Focused HR Service Technologies

Even more importantly, Pfau and Kay also report that there is a significant relationship between employee commitment (via the Employee Commitment Index or ECI) and shareholder value.

Relationship Between Employee Commitment and Shareholder Value

ECI Score	3-Year Total Return To Shareholders	
Low		76%
Average		90%
High		112%

Bean counters – snap to! Here's something you can dig your financial teeth into.

Leaders actually have the biggest impact on employee commitment in any organization. Pfau and Kay provide the proof. One of the key drivers of employee commitment according to their findings is "Trust in senior leadership." Consider the following table.

Trust In Senior Leadership And Employee Commitment

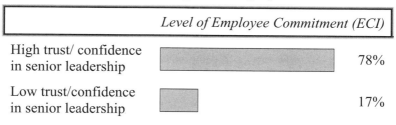

	Level of Employee Commitment (ECI)
High trust/ confidence in senior leadership	78%
Low trust/confidence in senior leadership	17%

If "Trust in senior leadership" helps build employee commitment, does employee commitment contribute to shareholder value? You better believe it does.

Trust In Senior Leadership And Shareholder Value

	3-Year Total Return To Shareholders
High trust/ confidence in senior leadership	108%
Low trust/confidence in senior leadership	66%

High trust and confidence in leadership attributed to 108 percent of shareholder value creation over three years versus a 66 percent return where there is low trust and confidence in leadership. That 42 percent difference makes it very clear that building strong relationships with people is a winning strategy for all leaders… senior, junior or anywhere in between.

The Creative Economy

The data from these recent studies on human capital may be impressive but it really shouldn't be surprising. Until now, invention has been the driver of humanity throughout the ages. We came up with the wheel so skateboards could conquer the sidewalks of our cities. We figured out how to harness lightning so that we could reheat our pizzas. We put our footprints on the surface of the same moon that controls our tides. Until machines begin making their own offspring, we, as humans, hold the key to invention within the power of our imaginings.

No one person develops anything completely on his or her own. Advancement comes from building on the knowledge of one another. One lab-coated scientist didn't get us to the moon – an army of them did. However, there are usually one or two people standing out in front pointing to an impossible goal and helping motivate and guide those behind them to make that goal a reality. That's you, the leader.

Business Week magazine coined the phrase "The Creative Economy" meaning that human creativity has become the key driver of growth in today's economy. We couldn't agree more. And it is your job as a leader to spur creativity, innovation and impossible dreams in those around you.

Should They All Be Committed?

To get your creative economy to work for you, you know you need that commitment. That's not all that hard to get, is it? Well, it's getting harder.

Recently, in USA Today, Stephanie Armour reports that in 2005, 42 percent of workers are "somewhat" to "very likely" to look for a new job in the coming year. In fact, within the article, Marc Lewis, North American president of Morgan Howard Worldwide (an executive search firm) is quoted to say "In 2005, companies that don't take care of their employees are going to see people leave."

Well, you're never going to get things done if your people keep leaving. And the thought of turnover costs can make even the most successful businessperson wince. When it comes to the people who work with and for you, they should all be committed. Otherwise, you'll never reach your goals.

Stop Pounding and Start Compounding

Hopefully we have provided enough evidence to convince any one needing convincing that a strong focus on "people" leadership is a good idea. The "beatings will continue until morale improves" days are over… and really should never have been a reality in the first place. So, we want to offer you a new motto… stop pounding [your people] and start compounding.

Our financial friends would tell us that the best way to make capital work for you is through compounding. For example, if you have $1,000 that you were looking to invest in a simple interest fund for the next 50 years at a rate of 10 percent, at the end of the 50 years you would have earned $6,000.

Take that same scenario but switch it to a fund that uses compounding interest and during that same 50 years, your $1,000 investment would earn you $117,390.85. A reasonably good return, wouldn't you say? Perhaps that is why "compound interest" is the 8th Wonder of the World.

Investment = $1,000
Time Frame = 50 years
Interest Rate = 10%

Simple Interest	Compound Interest
$1,000 over 50 years =	$1,000 over 50 years =
$6,000	$117,390.85

Well, human capital has the *potential* to compound, as well. We learn all the time: on the job, off the job, through formal education, through observation, through formal and informal feedback, through direct and indirect consequences to our actions, etc. We build up (compound) these experiences in order to create new ideas and knowledge that set us up for future experiences.

The problem with compounding human capital is that it can go either way: adding value or subtracting value. As a leader, you can either contribute to the value of those who work with you (compound their human capital) or you can detract from their value (pound their human capital). If you treat people like you value them and what they have to offer, you'll get a return on your investment that you would not believe.

So, we ask you again, do you think people are:

☐ Productive and imaginative
☐ Lazy and dull

Do your actions and interactions with people reflect your beliefs?

If you said that people were in large part "productive and imaginative," then you are ready to move on and can start learning how you can compound human capital for yourself and those you lead. The trick is to get people to want to give more, learn more, and create more.

This book is all about maximizing human capital for yourself and for those you lead. We are first going to show you that you (and everyone around you) is actually living in an invisible prison of your own making. We'll show you how this prison was built in the first place, how you can start to see it and how you can BreakOUT of it for yourself. Then, we'll move onto how you can actually help others BreakOUT by examining the basics of human behavior and how it can be used to encourage BreakOUT. Finally, we'll provide a nice long list of practices (BreakOUT Human Capital Practices) that can get you started and on your way to BreakOUT for your team.

BREAKOUT

But, first, let's begin with what BreakOUT really means and why we need to do it.

Part I:

B<small>REAK</small>OUT

People, Prisons and PCC's

BreakOUT

Chapter 1
Why BreakOUT?
(The Great Escape)

The idea of BreakOUT assumes one thing. It assumes that most of us – you, me, your family, your friends, your co-workers, your boss, your dentist and the guy who cuts you off in traffic – are all locked up in a prison of our own making. This prison both keeps the chaos of the outside world out and traps us inside. It both protects and prohibits. It is a highly secured environment that often hides us from potential and opportunity.

Most of us don't know that we're in this prison. If we did, the most natural questions would be, "What is it?" and "How did we get here?" The answers are even more troubling. Our prison consists of the boundaries and limitations we have placed on our lives and we are imprisoned within those boundaries by our own choosing. We consciously and unconsciously sentence ourselves to life-long internment in a prison of our own making.

The concept of BreakOUT is about unleashing the power of people, including your own power. To do this, you have to recognize this prison for what it is and how it impacts what you do (and don't do) – how you think, behave, act and react.

How often have you heard the phrase, "Think out of the box?" Our prison is our box. It is the patterns of thought and behavior that we have used to script our lives. We need this construct to help us function day-to-day in a big wide world full of the dangerous unknown. If we had to relearn how we brush our teeth, put our clothes on and how to drive to work as if it were a totally new experience each day, we wouldn't get anywhere. There are so many things that we do each day that we don't give conscious thought to; thankfully they are automatic so that we can designate our mental, physical and emotional resources to other things. The idea of having to learn how to tie our shoes every day from scratch is not an appealing one.

However, while this structure of patterned thoughts and behaviors serves us well most of the time, it is also the number one thing that holds most of us back both as individuals and as organizations. We can only see our lives and our world from the view behind the barred windows of our perceptions and expectations… and our view is limited to what we *think* we know about the world and ourselves. Consider the captain in the following story told by a former naval officer.

Two battleships assigned to a training squadron had been at sea on maneuvers in heavy weather for several days. I was serving on the lead battleship and was on watch on the bridge as night fell. The visibility was poor with patchy fog, so the captain remained on the bridge keeping an eye on all activity.

Shortly after dark, the lookout on the wing of the bridge reported, "Light bearing off the starboard bow."

"Is it steady or moving astern?" the captain called out.

Lookout replied, "Steady, captain," which meant we were on a dangerous collision course with that ship.

The captain then called to the signalman, "Signal that ship: We are on a dangerous collision course, advise you change course 20 degrees."

Back came a signal, "Advisable for YOU to change course 20 degrees."

The captain said, "Send: I'm a captain, change course 20 degrees."

"I'm a seaman second class," came the reply. "YOU had better change course 20 degrees."

By this time the captain was furious. He spat out, "Send: I'm a battleship. Change course 20 degrees!"

Back came the flashing light. "I'm a lighthouse!"

We changed course.

Our prison is made up of expectations and conditioned responses. But when expectations and conditions change, it can completely shift how we view the world and how we act and react to it. Usually, this shift causes a strong emotional reaction inside. In the case of the captain, he most likely felt anger and then frustration or embarrassment when he eventually had to change course.

In order to live out our daily lives with any measure of peace and security, a certain amount of structure and order must exist. Even in chaos, there is some kind of order – even if only an understanding that everything will be completely unpredictable. But for most of us, chaos is something we try and avoid at all costs.

Great Expectations

When we turn on a water faucet, we expect the water to begin to flow. If it doesn't, we face a myriad of possible emotions and reactions. We can at first be startled and then perplexed, trying the hot and cold knobs several times just to be sure what we expect to happen really isn't happening. Then, within us the faucet of uncertainty begins to flow. We can get angry and/or be frustrated (especially if we have a head full of shampoo). Or, we could get scared and/or feel helpless (especially when there is not a plumber in sight).

When things we expect to happen don't, we are initially lost (even if just for a moment). We have conditioned ourselves to expect certain things in our lives to be real or unreal, possible or impossible, natural or unnatural, so that we can plan and arrange our lives. *But that which creates order can also limit potential.* If we are conditioned to think only certain things are possible and that there are only certain ways things can be done, then we close ourselves to other opportunities and possibilities.

Consider this. If you take a jar and fill it with some flies and put a lid on it for a few days, what would happen when you take the lid off the jar? Very few flies would leave the jar. Why? The flies have become so used to their prison that they don't even realize that they are inside of it... and that they now have an option to leave. Even if some of the flies did realize that they could escape, there would be an initial struggle between old fears of what might be out there and the new opportunity their freedom might award them.

The same is true for many of us. If you have been in prison for most of your life and all of the sudden, the door swings open and you are able to move freely throughout the wide, wild, world, how would you react?

B<small>REAK</small>OUT

Organizational Prisons

The problem is not limited to individuals. When we get together in groups, the same types of prisons can be built up. Organizations can also get stuck in certain patterns of thinking and doing that limit its potential. So, as you put people together, they not only face their individual box, but are imprisoned in the group box, as well.

The ability to BreakOUT takes a certain amount of "brainery" and a whole lot of bravery. BreakOUT takes a bold person (or company)… people willing to grab the keys of courage, commitment and creativity and unlock the door of the mind. For you as an individual, BreakOUT takes a certain level of fearlessness and doggedness. As a leader trying to help others BreakOUT of their individual prisons, it takes a strong understanding of how people think and act in order to help set them free.

So, what's the big deal about BreakOUT? If the prison can be a comfortable, safe place from which to view the world, why try and BreakOUT at all? What's in it for you?

Butterfly BreakOUT

In 1973, a film starring Steve McQueen and Dustin Hoffman was released entitled *Papillon*. The movie was based on the life story of Henri "Papillon" Charriere, a Frenchman convicted of murder in 1931. Still claiming his innocence, Papillon

(French for "butterfly,") was sent to the feared penal colonies on the coast of French Guiana. The prison system was made up of various high security settlements both on the coast and the surrounding islands. Not only were the prison conditions harsh in and of themselves, but also hot, humid temperatures and the realities of living in the African jungle were terrifying. Those inmates who survived their initial sentence were forced to remain in Guiana as exiles for an equal period of time, but 90 percent of them died of malaria or yellow fever before ever having the chance to return home.

In the film, Papillon (played by Steve McQueen) made it very clear from the outset that his only goal – his mission – was to escape. While others around him bemoaned their situation and/or tried to make the best of their incarceration by seeking coveted prison jobs and working the inmate black market, Papillon thought only about how he could break out.

During his incarceration, Papillon befriended the famed counterfeiter Louis Degas (played by Dustin Hoffman). Louis, too, wanted his freedom but his hopes rested on working through more conventional legal channels to prove his innocence and lessen his term. This was understandable given the fact that no one had ever successfully escaped from any of the French Guiana prison settlements and lived to tell about it.

The penalty for even trying to break out was extremely severe. Two years of solitary confinement were added to a prisoner's sentence for the first attempt. A second escape attempt would earn a prisoner five years in solitary confinement. If the silence and seclusion didn't get to them, then the near starvation and mental stress would. Solitary confinement was not meant to rehabilitate an inmate… it was meant to break him.

Papillon's first escape attempt ended quickly and earned him his first two years in solitary confinement, which he survived with the help of his friend Louis who sneaked him extra food. Once out of his nearly fatal term in solitary, Papillon once again built up his strength and again made his plans to escape.

Louis agreed to help plan Papillon's second escape but honestly had no intention of going with him; Louis still believed his pleas via the legal system would earn him his release. However, just as Papillon was jumping the wall of the compound, a guard saw Louis helping Papillon to escape and Louis was forced to join in the break out. Unfortunately for them both, they were again recaptured with Louis getting his two years and Papillon earning his five years locked in the silence of their small, dank, solitary cells.

Finally, incredibly aged by hardship and malnutrition, Papillon and Louis were both sent to the Devil's Island penal colony to live out the rest of their lives. Devil's Island was aptly named, needing few guards or fences. Primarily a mass of rocks in the middle of the swirling sea, one small boat dock cut into a cliff side was the only way on or off the island. As a guard told

Papillon when he arrived, "The tides and the sharks do the rest."

There were no prison buildings on the island and there were no cells. Indeed, Devil's Island inmates lived in relative luxury and freedom – each having their own hut and small pieces of land to do with as they pleased. There was no intent to incarcerate or punish… the prisoners on Devil's Island were left there to be forgotten forever.

Louis, mentally broken by his years in solitary confinement, found a measure of peace on Devil's Island by being given seeds to plant and grow a garden. Papillon, despite everything he had endured, remained restless and was still driven by his dreams of escape. One day, he convinced Louis to take time out from his gardening and come to the edge of one of the cliffs above the churning sea. At this particular part of the island, a horseshoe shaped opening had been cut into the cliffs by the powerful surge of waves that were constantly battering the island before they were forced back out to sea.

Papillon suggested to Louis that if a person were to jump out far enough with a raft made out of large bags filled with coconuts, it could be possible to catch the current and float out to sea. It was a mere 24 miles to the mainland and Papillon was captivated with the idea that they could actually be free men within two days. Louis, ever the supportive friend, agreed that he would go with Papillon and together they filled a single bag with coconuts to test Papillon's theory.

B<small>REAK</small>OUT

Once again at the cliff's edge, Papillon threw the bag into the air and they both watched it fall the long way down to the ocean below. The waves picked up the bag, started to carry it out to sea only to sweep it back toward shore, viciously throwing it up against the rocks where it smashed to pieces.

Louis looked at his friend sympathetically and tottered off to care for the tomatoes in his garden. Papillon remained at the cliff's edge and stared unwaveringly at the water below still unwilling to give up his dream… to breakout and escape from Devil's Island.

Weeks passed and Papillon once again visited Louis in his garden. As excited as a child, Papillon pronounced, "It was the wrong wave!" He had watched the waves come in and recede from the cove over and over again and discovered a pattern. Every seventh wave was a really big wave… powerful enough to carry them out to sea and away from the rocks. Once again, Louis joined his friend at the edge of freedom with two rafts made of bags filled with coconuts.

Papillon was ready to break out. He eagerly counted the waves… 1, 2, 3, 4, 5… and told Louis to get ready to throw his raft. Louis steps back. He looked at his friend, the dreamer, and stated quietly, "I really meant to go." Papillon nodded back to Louis in understanding. He realized that while part of Louis wanted to break out, another part of Louis never really believed break out was possible. Louis had indulged his friend and fed upon Papillon's hope and courage… but, in the end, he himself never really believed he could ever be free.

Papillon said goodbye to Louis and leapt into the ocean below. Louis smiled as he watched a dark spot riding a wave out to sea and then, with a shake of his head, walked back to his garden. The final scene of the film showed Henri "Papillon" Charriere still very much alive and cursing his captors as he floated off to freedom. The butterfly had successfully made his break out – living out the remainder of his years as a free man in Venezuela.

A Personal Revolution

BreakOUT is a personal revolution… a decision to acknowledge the boundaries that help keep you safe and sane… and also see how in many cases they can hold you back from reaching for your dreams. Your personal revolt might not be of the same scale as Papillon but it probably does not need to be.

Each one of us has something we have wanted to do or wanted to be that we have not yet been able to realize. We all have in us a measure of under-utilized potential; of personal power yet to be unleashed that we don't quite know how to tap. That potential is our call to freedom. That is our call to BreakOUT.

And, while each of us can seek BreakOUT for ourselves, as leaders, we can also help motivate and drive others to seek

B<small>REAK</small>OUT

BreakOUT for themselves. We can surpass our friend Papillon and help the Louis' of the world unleash their power and potential, as well. This idea of BreakOUT can be powerful both for us and for those we lead.

As we have said, just as individuals build prisons, groups of people build prisons, too. That means groups of people can BreakOUT together, as well. Consider the story of Baptist Health Care in Pensacola, Florida.

The Baptist Story

In 1996, Baptist Health Care had to face some really hard facts. Employee turnover was over 30 percent. Even worse, patient satisfaction scores had dropped to the 18th percentile.

They were in trouble and knew things had to change. They were in a prison of their own making and staying where they were was no longer an option. They say that change happens when you either "feel the heat or see the light." Baptist Health Care was definitely feeling the heat to BreakOUT.

But, then, something remarkable happened. Within the span of one year, they were able to bring patient satisfaction scores from their low at 18th percentile up to the 99th percentile – the top 1 percent of all hospitals. In 2003, Baptist Health Care celebrated its success with employee turnover sinking steadily to 13.9 percent and with patient satisfaction scores consistently in the 99th percentile.

Baptist Health Care is now consistently one of the companies on Fortune's "100 Best Companies To Work For" list. In 2004, they achieved their greatest achievement to date. Baptist Health Care won the coveted Malcolm Baldrige National Quality Award award.

The rest of this book will focus on how you can unleash the power of people – freeing yourself, your team and your organization from the prison of "perceived" limitations. It's your choice. It's time to BreakOUT. So, if you want to unleash your power and the power of others, turn the page to take the first step toward BreakOUT.

BreakOUT

Chapter 2
Premature Cognition
(BreakOUT Of The Blocks)

Picture your prison. What does it look like? What is it made of? What are its strongest and weakest points? How can we use those weaknesses to help plan our BreakOUT?

To begin to answer these questions, we need to understand how and why the prison was built in the first place.

Premature Cognitive Commitments (PCC's)

Think about everything you do in a day. It's a pretty long list. You might start by swinging your legs out of bed, standing up and then you possibly… shower, dress, walk, talk, cook, eat, clean, drive, dial, read, write, sit, hug, smile, stir, listen, open, close, lift, mix, start, stop, and possibly even program the VCR. How is it that you know how to do all of these things? Most likely, it is because you have done them before.

Now, imagine if tonight, from the time you went to bed at night to the time you wake up tomorrow, you forgot how to do any and all of these things… that you had to start tomorrow without any memory from the previous day. You would have to learn how to do the simplest things from the beginning. Think of just how little we all would accomplish in our lives if we had to start from scratch each day.

We are creatures of learning. Through experience and practice we gain many degrees of knowledge that becomes ingrained in our minds. This ingrained knowledge becomes so much a part of our thinking that it grows to be "natural" or "automatic" behavior.

The practice of driving a car can be so entrenched that most of us perform the hundreds of tasks to get us from home to work and back again without much conscious thought. You don't think about pushing the gas pedal down when a light turns green or turning the steering wheel to make a turn. You just do it automatically. Similarly, if it is a cloudy day, we might think it natural to take an umbrella because we have learned that clouds equate to rain. When we flick on a light switch, it seems natural to expect the lights to go on.

We are taught by our experiences that certain things are true, natural and we come to expect them. In psychology, these types of thoughts are called *premature cognitive commitments (PCC's)*. PCC's mean that we typically will act on what the memory of past experience has taught us. We know what we know based on past experience and it affects our current behavior. PCC's provide the framework to help us live out our daily lives automatically – without starting from scratch every time we face the dawn.

To better understand premature cognitive commitment, let's break the term down.

Premature – happening, arriving, or existing prior to adequate diagnosis, analysis or consideration.

Cognitive – to become acquainted with; to know: the act or process of knowing including both awareness and judgment.

Commitment – a relatively permanent opinion or mindset that filters the information we receive and shapes how we act.

So, the three words – premature, cognitive and commitment – combine to explain why we often jump to a conclusion or idea without giving it our full consideration or analysis. And again, we develop our PCC's based on our past experience.

Naturally, by basing our actions on our past experiences, we are limiting ourselves to only what we have done before. This is where the prison comes in. While our prison of past experience can help us get efficiently through the day, it also limits us as to what we "think" we can and cannot do. In other words, PCC's both help and hinder.

B<small>REAK</small>OUT

How PCC's Help

As we mentioned before, if we had to relearn everything we know at the start of each day, we really would never progress as either individuals or as a people. In order to prevent this, we have the ability to develop patterns of thought that allow certain knowledge to be fixed in order for us to build upon it. This PCC framework places boundaries or limits on how we think about things.

Now, most people when they hear the words "boundary" or "limitation" immediately perceive them in a negative way (which is a PCC within itself). But, limitations are very natural and valuable things.

You perceive everything through one of five sense windows – sight, hearing, taste, touch, and smell. If your senses aren't impaired, they operate twenty-four hours a day. Consider what science tells you about these senses.

Light is a form of electromagnetic wave. Light waves travel through space at 186,000 miles per second. And you see light. Radar, radio signals, and x-rays are also electromagnetic waves. They also travel at 186,000 miles per second. But you don't see them. Although you might want to see radar signals transmitted from police cars, physical limitations do not allow you to do so. So you buy a radar detector, mount it on the dashboard of your car, and let it "see" for you.

The simple fact is that light waves account for less than 2 percent of all those electromagnetic waves rushing past you at this moment. Imagine how muddled your mind would be if you could see the electromagnetic waves emerging from radio stations in your community or the radar waves emitted from planes flying overhead.

Sound also travels in wave patterns. These wave patterns vibrate, and you hear them. "Normal" hearing means that you can hear sound waves that vibrate between 15 and 15,000 times a second. In older people who are experiencing some hearing loss, the upper limit drops to around 4,000. Among young children, the upper limit can be as high as 30,000. Thus, they hear better than you do as an adult, although any parent will likely testify that his or her child is an exception!

If you could hear sound waves that vibrate fewer than 15 times per second, then, like a robin, you could hear earthworms moving beneath the ground. But you'd also hear your muscles expand and contract as you move your arms and legs. And you'd be plagued by the sound of your blood rushing through your veins and arteries.

Bats use echolocation with sound waves that vibrate between 50,000 and 90,000 times a second to locate things, such as cave walls, tiny insects, and your house. If there are bats in your neighborhood (or in your attic), then you'd be absolutely miserable if you could hear better than the average human because you could hear their cacophony of sounds all the time.

Physical limitations affect your other senses as well. For example, most birds have a wonderfully keen sense of hearing but almost no sense of smell. Yet the human sense of smell is finely developed and often the only difference between French cuisine and an ordinary meal is the impact that food has on the olfactory receptors inside your nose. This is because we can taste only bitter, sweet, salty, and sour. Actually, when we eat, all five senses come together. Maybe that's why some of us enjoy mealtime so much.

So nature's physical limitations help us perceive better because we don't need to perceive everything. Although you might sometimes want to remove these limitations, they normally keep you from being overloaded with sensory information.

As you read this right now, you are probably filtering out several things around you… people talking, the feel of the clothes against your body, the flow of air through your nostrils as you breath in and out. You could never focus on reading if you didn't limit your awareness to exclude other things going on in and around you.

So, the fact that we all walk around with mental limitations as to how we think and what we do is very natural. It's a protective process to help us deal with everyday life. However, the same walls that help protect us also close us in by not letting us see what else might be out there.

How PCC's Hinder

There you sit reading this book and without knowing it, a friend of yours comes behind you and taps you on the shoulder. You jump out of your seat. Your limited perception of the world, for the moment being the text on this page, didn't let you sense your friend's approach. The same thing can happen on a much larger scale.

For instance, we have a friend who shared with us how his PCC's kept him from taking advantage of many opportunities he was offered in his life. When he was a young child, he overheard his mother talking to a friend about his father. His father had recently moved out because he and our friend's mother were having marital problems. Specifically, the father had been out of work for several months and when he said he was out looking for work, he had actually been spending time with another woman.

In a fit of anger, our friend's mother told her friend, "With such a loser as a father, [our friend] will probably turn out the same way!" Our friend told us that this started a pattern of thought of what he could expect to achieve in life. When other seniors were applying for college, he didn't even bother to fill out the paperwork. He persistently jumped ship whenever a relationship came close to a commitment. His PCC's told him that he "couldn't" be successful... so his behaviors reflected this mental reality.

As we said before, PCC's also exist within groups of people. In his book *Mastering the Dynamics of Innovation*, James Utterback tells the story of the American ice industry in New England in the late 1800's. You see, back then, companies would cut ice from frozen lakes and ship it all over the world. Most of the ice would melt on the way, but they deliberately cut enough to make sure what did make it was enough to earn a profit.

But, soon came the age of mechanical ice makers. Companies no longer needed to cut ice out of frozen lakes because they could make their own ice in 150 pound blocks. So the ice harvesters lost their business to ice makers. But, the ice makers didn't get to hang on long because refrigeration was just around the corner. Everyone could now make ice cubes in their homes.

Why did the ice harvesters (and later ice makers) go out of business? Why didn't they just switch from cutting ice from lakes to selling machines that make ice? They didn't because the prison of what they had always done before trapped them. They were ice harvesters. Better saws, better storage and faster transportation were what were going to keep them competitive.

But, the "BreakOUT" idea to switch from what they had always done (harvesting ice) to something entirely new (building ice makers) wasn't perceived as a "realistic" option. So, despite all their efforts, they went out of business – they fell victim to their premature cognitive commitments.

Another example comes from the Swiss. In 1960, 85 percent to 90 percent of all wristwatches came from Switzerland. Swiss mainspring watches were considered to be of the highest quality and workmanship in the world. They were THE wristwatches to own.

A few years later, two Swiss engineers invented the quartz movement. Despite their enthusiasm and confidence that this was a whole new market for the industry, no one in their country would even consider producing a digital watch. The Swiss mainspring watchmakers rejected the quartz movement as a technology without a future. Swiss watchmakers would never sully their reputation with such an inferior watch.

So, the engineers decided to take their technology elsewhere – specifically to Seiko in Japan. The Swiss quickly realized what they had been blinded to… especially when they only held 8 percent of the watch market and 40,000 Swiss mainspring watchmakers were unemployed within 2 years.

Again, their premature cognitive commitments told them that they didn't need to make dramatically different watches because the old ones had always done so well. Their PCC "prison" kept them from seeing new opportunity when it knocked on their door. When PCC's become this strong it might be more appropriate to call them Premature Cognitive Mindsets. Mindsets so strong that no matter how "smart" we are, we are blinded to other real opportunities.

Small Steps Versus Big Giant Leaps

PCC's keep us from thinking big. Like the ice harvesters or watchmakers, we all tend to settle for making small improvements or enhancements instead of taking great leaps of innovation. We'll choose to lose 5 pounds over becoming a tri-athlete. We'll settle for an okay job over the job of our dreams. We'll tweak our lives instead of going full blast.

> *Strategy is frequently about trying to*
> *continue the past in some imagined future.*
> *BreakOUT is about creating the future.*

Albert Einstein is quoted as saying the definition of insanity is "doing the same thing over and over again and expecting different results." Yet, so many of us do exactly that when we try and improve our lives. We expect our past experiences (and the PCC's they created within us) to determine our future. But if that were truly the way of things, none of us would have ever taken that first monumental step as a child. And, that first step led us out the door and into the world… a world that we can change if we choose to.

Think back to our friend, Papillon. Papillon could have chosen to make small improvements to his situation. He could have, like his friend, Louis, chosen to plant tomatoes as a way to enrich his existence on Devil's Island. But Papillon made a choice... he chose to believe that he could be free. He didn't let "little" PCC's like the fact that no one had ever escaped the French Guiana prison system alive before deter him from his goal. Papillon made a great leap off a really big cliff. And, he caught a really big wave to freedom.

That's our challenge, as well. How do we catch the "seventh wave?" We need to stop thinking incrementally and start thinking transformationally.

PCC's and Emotions

Our individual and group PCC's are tough to see. Not only have they become so natural to us that we are blinded to them, but also because they are reinforced and magnified by our emotions. Strong emotions can take reality and forcibly mold it into something that fits into our existing mental framework.

If you've ever visited a turkey farm, then you know turkeys are not very smart. During thunderstorms, some turkeys literally don't have sense enough to come in out of the rain. Instead, they tilt their heads back, open their beaks and drink until they drown. When frightened by thunder, turkeys will all rush to one corner of their pen for protection. The problem is, they all tend to rush to the same corner, sometimes resulting in a feathered pile of crushed and smothered turkeys.

Even though they're not very smart, female turkeys tend to be good mothers, but only if something very specific triggers that mothering reaction. They diligently watch and protect their young, spending much of their time warming their chicks beneath their wings. This behavior apparently is triggered by a distinctive, high-pitched "cheep, cheep" sound young turkeys make. It's that precise sound which makes the difference. A young turkey's smell, appearance or touch plays almost no role in eliciting a mother's protective behavior. In fact, if a baby turkey for some reason doesn't make that "cheep, cheep" sound, the mother will abandon or, in some cases, kill the chick. That "cheep cheep" sound triggers a PCC in the mother turkey that results in a number of "automatic" mothering behaviors.

The mother turkey's almost total reliance on that single sound for identifying her young can and does produce some strange behavior. The animal behaviorist, M.S. Fox, did an experiment with mother turkeys and a stuffed skunk. Skunks are a natural enemy of turkeys. Generally, whenever a skunk approaches, a mother turkey will flap her wings, squawk, peck and claw at the skunk to drive it away. Fox's experiment showed that the mother turkeys would react that way even toward a stuffed skunk, pulled by a string toward a mother turkey – until the tape recorder inside the stuffed skunk made a "cheep, cheep" sound.

Then, the mother turkey would stop her violent attacks and even occasionally try to draw the skunk under her wing. But as soon as the tape recorder was turned off and the "cheep, cheep" stopped, the mother turkey would attack once again.

This experiment shows that we should all be grateful that, as human beings, we are able to think, understand, and perceive the world around us better than any mother turkey. Don't we?

Consider the following four questions:

Question 1:   How many people in the United States die each year of skin cancer? 9,600 – yet most of us continue to sunbathe.

Question 2:   How many people in the United States die each year in auto accidents? Nearly 41,821 (with 3,189,000 people injured) – yet 86 percent of the population 15 years and older have driver's licenses.

Question 3:   How many people in the United States die each year of diseases related to smoking? More than 430,000 – yet approximately 46.2 million Americans continue to smoke (with 3,000 young people becoming smokers every day).

Question 4:   How many swimmers die each year from shark attacks WORLDWIDE? – Four people in 2003 (only one of which was in the U.S.). The average for the new millennium is three deaths per year… worldwide.

Armed with these statistics, the next time you are near the
ocean, walk down to the beach and gingerly step over all the
people lying there soaking up the sun's rays and scorching their
skin. Wade into the surf until it gets about knee-high. Then, at
the top of your lungs, yell two words. No, it's not "cheep
cheep." It's "Shark! Shark!" Then stand back and watch the
"turkeys…"

- Scramble out of the water

- Stumble over the sunbathers

- Jump into their cars

- Light up a cigarette

- Then drive to safety

OK, you know you won't actually try this little experiment, but
you get the point. People are susceptible to what we call
"Shark Syndrome Perception." Despite having a finely tuned
capacity for understanding the world around them, people often
perceive only what they want to about their surroundings, no
matter what the facts are and despite the efforts of reasonable
people to convince them otherwise.

> *PCC's make it difficult to BreakOUT.*
> *When strong emotions are attached to*
> *PCC's, it becomes almost impossible!*

Sharks are considered to be big, mean and have lots of really sharp teeth. They are scary. Because they incite the emotion of fear within us, we perceive them to be a far greater threat to human life than cigarettes, driving a car and skin cancer – even though the facts prove quite the opposite. We have a premature cognitive commitment that sharks are out to get us and our fear backs this up. So, it powerfully affects how we think and act.

Why It's Hard To BreakOUT

Here comes the big question. You now understand that PCC's can both help and hinder you, filtering out many things that would distract you but also blinding you to certain opportunities and/or dangers coming your way. But, now that you know, what's next? How are you supposed to BreakOUT of prison that you can't really see? When people tell you to think out of the box – or BreakOUT of your PCC prison – how are you supposed to start? Well, we'll start to answer this question by looking at how some other people do it.

In his book *Lighting in a Bottle*, David Baum tells us about the Mescalero Apache. They are infamous for their ability to seem invisible, able to blend into any environment and be unseen by the enemy. Out in the open, they have been known to remain completely undetected as whole regimens of U.S. soldiers rode by.

They don't use camouflage or illusion. How do they do it? A Mescalero Apache elder shared the secret with Baum. "We move in the negative space," he said. The elder goes on to explain it in this way. Imagine you were looking out to an isolated grove of trees. What would you see? You would probably see the trees, some underbrush and perhaps a few rocks. But what is between the trees, brush and rocks? What would you see there?

The answer is nothing. That is "negative space." It is space that lies between the things we do see. We never really notice the in-between – just the things that we can identify. "That is the secret to our invisibility," says the elder. "We stay in the negative space where we won't be noticed."

And it is in this negative space that the secret to BreakOUT is hidden between the bars of our prison cell. The first thing we have to accept is that, there are always ways for us to BreakOUT of our PCC prison. There is a lot of negative space within the walls we have built up around ourselves. We have to acknowledge that there are other options, possibilities, and opportunities available to us *that we might not yet be able to see*. That acknowledgment is how we begin to work towards BreakOUT.

The other factor that is absolutely imperative to helping BreakOUT is a drive to do it. It's more than "wanting" to get out of our prison, it's "needing" to.

Feel The Heat, See The Light

There is a saying that all change comes from either "feeling the heat or seeing the light." Back in 1988, Andy Mochan was working as a superintendent on the Piper Alpha oil-drilling platform off the coast of Scotland. One night after Andy had gone to sleep, there was a terrible explosion and fire on the platform. Andy rushed out of his room at the sound of the alarms and managed to get to the edge of the platform. Behind him was a wall of fire and below him, a churning sea of debris and pools of ignited oil. Andy knew that if he survived the 15-story fall to the ocean below, the frigid waters would kill him within minutes. Andy jumped… and he survived.

In the end, the explosion on the Piper Alpha claimed one hundred and sixty-six crew and two rescuers in what was heralded as the worst catastrophe in the twenty-five year history of North Sea oil exploration. Later, when he was asked why he made a potentially fatal leap, Andy replied, "It was either jump or fry."

Andy literally felt the heat. Maintaining the status quo – staying on the platform was no longer an option for Andy. Nor is it an option for many of us. Doing what we have always done, over and over again, won't get us anywhere but stuck.

*Our "historic competencies" are
frequently irrelevant to our future.*

You see, Andy was lucky in more than just having survived. Normally, he would never have even considered jumping from the platform to the waters below. He would have considered it to be suicide. Everything in his brain would have told him not to do it. But there was a fire. He didn't have any other choice. Staying where he was would have meant certain death.

Most of us don't have a fire telling us that what we think is impossible might not be. You might be saying to yourself, "Well, my beliefs aren't so dangerous that they'll get me killed." Maybe. Maybe not. If your current PCC's tell you that it is okay to smoke, have an unhealthy diet, drive fast or swim with sharks, you could indeed be in danger.

But even if this isn't the case, an even more sinister fire is burning. It is the threat of living a life half-lived. What is holding you back from fulfilling your dreams? What is stopping you from reaching your highest measure of success... in your career, your relationships, your physique, and in your life?

For groups, what is stopping you from reaching the top? When other teams are winning the prize, why aren't you?

That's your motivation to BreakOUT. You have to "see the light" as to how things could be versus how they currently are. Your potential future is the catalyst that will inspire you to make the effort to identify the PCC's you are imprisoned by and to search in the negative space of your life for different and new ways to think, act and live.

If you have the desire to BreakOUT, keep reading. The next chapter will help you identify some of your PCC's so that you can begin your work toward your release from PCC prison.

B<small>REAK</small>OUT

Chapter 3
Know Thyself!
(BreakOUT Thru Self-Discovery)

A woman we work with, actually the one who is typing this manuscript, has a bumper sticker on the back of her car that says: ***Begin Within***.

This is excellent advice... especially in terms of working toward personal BreakOUT. If you want to BreakOUT, it's kind of a good idea to know what you are "in" first. What does your prison look like? How big is it? Is it well guarded? What are the bars made of? Most importantly, what tools are accessible to you to help you escape? BreakOUT can't happen if you have no idea what prison you're in.

Well, when it comes to breaking out of our own PCC's, the self becomes the object of study. It's understanding how and why you think, act and react the way you do that becomes your first key to BreakOUT. What are your strengths, your weaknesses, your likes, your dislikes, the things you can do, the things you can't, and the things you've never yet tried?

BreakOUT

Now, you know who you are, don't you? Sure you do. Here's how you can prove it to yourself. Give yourself three minutes, *and only three minutes*, to answer the following questions.

- My name is _____. (Okay, so far, so good.)
- If I were to describe the "real" me in 10 words or less, it would read, I am _____.
- My main purpose in life is _____.
- If you are 45 years old or older, answer this last question. When I leave this world, people will remember me for _____.

You were able to easily answer the questions within the time limit right? Maybe not. Contrary to what you might think, most people don't really know exactly who they are and what their purpose is. For varied reasons, most of us end up going through life with very little conscious thought about what it is we are actually trying to accomplish (if anything, in deference to certain of our existentialist friends). We run around on automatic pilot. We go to work, spend time with family and friends, go to the gym or the store, or the bank… drycleaners… church… whatever… and then come home again without a real sense of what it all means.

Now, we are very busy with all of these things. They monopolize the majority of our time, energy and focus. But how often do we actually question why we do all of the things we do. What real meaning or value do they have for us?

It is very easy to confuse activity with purpose, isn't it? Most of us have fallen into the pattern where the things we *do* in life *determine* our life. Self-awareness breaks this pattern. It allows us to take back control of what we do by knowing why we do them. Through self-awareness, we can stop *reacting* to life and start living it – deliberately.

The Significance of Self-Awareness

A lack of self-awareness becomes especially poignant when something catches us off guard and we just don't know what to do. For example, a friend recently told us that his wife came to him one day and just up and told him she wanted a divorce. She said she had had enough of his behavior and, since he wouldn't ask for one, she would. He was completely blindsided by her announcement. At that point, he honestly thought the marriage was a solid one.

Then, he told us, once he took some time to think about it, there were plenty of signs that things were going wrong long before his wife asked for the divorce. In fact, he realized that he himself had been unconsciously sabotaging the marriage in small ways for quite some time. When it came right down to it, he admitted to us (and himself) that he hadn't wanted to get married in the first place. He had just never taken the time to actually ask himself what it was he wanted from the relationship, whether the woman he was with wanted the same things, and what the best course of action would be (for both of them).

Our friend lacked self-awareness. He had been responding to situations in his life that he had created without any real thought about what he was doing and was making decisions that didn't connect with what it was he actually wanted out of life. He discovered why it is that self-awareness is so important... it stops the cycle of reacting to life and allows us to start pro-acting our life.

Self-aware·ness /'self – 'wer'nes/

1: an awareness of one's own personality, individuality or behaviors

When we are in a "reacting" frame of mind, we stay in jobs we don't like, relationships that aren't productive, or in situations and states that are unhealthy for our bodies, our minds and/or our spirits. When we are in a "pro-active and aware" state of mind, we are able to direct and guide our lives with far more purpose, able to get the things that we really value and want out of life.

If we want to BreakOUT... if we want to start actively living our lives instead of having our lives live us, we have to know what makes us tick. What is our role in making our lives what they are? Why is it that we do the things we do? The first step is to look at why it is actually difficult for us to see ourselves clearly. Why don't we ask the questions that logic would say are essential to answer before we get out of bed one more day? We have to deal with the Noise.

Turning Down The Volume To Pump Up Our Lives

In 1997, the *Journal of Applied Psychology* reported that high-performing managers can accurately rate their own performance, whereas average performing managers could not. This makes sense... high performing, more successful people have a more accurate and true sense of themselves. However, in that same study, it was also found that no matter how well a manager performed, they were still blind to knowing exactly what parts of their performance are more important to their ultimate success than others. In other words, even the most successful people still lacked self-awareness about what it is they do that gets them what they want.

A popular formula that is used to explain individual performance is **The Performance Equation**. It is a combination of factors that determines our current performance level and how we can improve that performance in the future.

$$\text{Individual Performance} = ((\text{Present Ability} + \text{Potential}) \times \text{Correct \& Consistent Practice}) - \text{Noise}$$

- **Present Ability:** Our present ability is primarily the skills, knowledge and know-how we currently have.

- **Potential:** Our potential is basically our talent – the skills we can tap into and/or what we can learn to help us achieve our greatest potential.

- **Correct & Consistent Practice:** The actions/behaviors we engage in that apply our present abilities and potential in a way that builds upon and reinforces these skills.

- **Noise:** Noise is basically all of things that distract us from being focused, accurately measuring and/or improving our performance.

There are two types of noise: external and internal. External noise can include the seemingly never-ending racket going on around us all the time: your kids arguing in the backseat on the way to school, your boss yelling about the lost report, your best friend's endless tirade on the cell phone about her latest dating saga, the radio, the television, the sound of your dog's snore at three in the morning.

Internal noise is the constant cacophony of ideas, thoughts and imaginings that flow through our minds during our every waking minute. Specifically, internal noise consists of those things that distract us from the inside out – concerns over family or other relationships, self-confidence issues, doubts, fears, etc.

To better understand the concept of noise, think about a professional basketball player at the free throw line. Behind the basket is a churning sea of literally hundreds of fans all jumping up and down, waving banners and yelling at the top of their lungs as the player prepares to take the shot. This is external noise.

As he takes his shot, the player knows that at his best, he has a 60 percent accuracy rating on his free throws for the season. He has already made 6 consecutive shots in this game. Can he do better than he has ever done and move to a new level of performance or will he miss the next four free throws? This is internal noise.

Step one to reducing noise in your life is to give yourself some quiet time, place and space. There are countless ways you can turn down the volume in your life: walk on the beach, pray, play golf, work in your garden, journal, cook, climb a mountain and talk to a billy goat. Whatever works for you. Do something… anything that will reduce the noise and give that opportunity to think about who you are, what you want and what, if anything, is stopping you from getting what you want.

Look inside… get some "in" sight about what you are all about. As you do, you'll start uncovering PCC's pretty much everywhere in your life – beliefs and ideas that have been limiting you for years – and you can start doing something about them.

First, we do have to warn you about one thing when it comes to self-awareness. Remember, that when you look into any mirror, your PCC's impact what you see and can sometimes give you a false image of you and your life. The fact of the matter is, we aren't always the best tool for our own self-discovery. It can help to get an outside perspective on things. Often, others can see us more clearly than we see ourselves. Indeed, others can really help us reflect on ourselves.

Mirror, Mirror… Off The Wall

From shrinks to bartenders to taxi drivers, all of us at one time or another probably asked a licensed professional (bartenders and taxi drivers have licenses, don't they?) for their take on something we were going through. Either that, or we have sought the input of a family member, friend or outside expert to help us understand what it is we should do in a particular situation. This tactic makes perfect sense when you look at it in terms of PCC's. If they are *your* Premature Cognitive Commitments, then it makes sense that it is hard for *you* to see them. But other people don't have the same blind spots we do and that, coupled with some experience and training, can set others up to be excellent mirrors to reflect who we are and what's going on in our lives.

A great example of this is a coach. Coaching of all types is rapidly gaining popularity. There are sports coaches, music coaches, career coaches, performance coaches, life coaches, etc… each working busily out there, right now. And, everyone from professional athletes to professional CEOs to first-time bowlers are making use of them. Why?

The reason is that coaches not only offer us that "outside" perspective to help heighten our self-awareness, but they also help us plan our escape from our current state to a better state.

In England in the 1500's, "a coach" referred to a particular type of carriage. This carriage took you from where you were to where you wanted to go. "To be coached" means pretty much the same thing, today. Being "coached" means that you are getting help to get from where you are to where you want to be. As the helpful "other" in this case, a coach can help us to become more self-aware based on his or her "outside" perspective and then pushes, pulls, motivates and celebrates us to make the changes we want in our lives.

So, if other people can reflect aspects of ourselves back to us, then it can be said that all relationships are exercises in self-awareness, right? Well, yes… if we want them to be. Any relationship can help us get a clearer picture of who we are. But, there is another whole, big, can of worms waiting to be opened here. When it comes to any group relationship, be it a group of two or two-thousand, you will see things your way, others will see things their way and the only way that *YOU* can have a clear picture of what's really going on is if you know *YOUR* stuff… and *THEIRS*. You have to see things from both sides of the glass.

B<small>REAK</small>OUT

The Johari Window: The Two-Way Awareness Mirror

Back in 1955, Joseph Luft and Harry Ingram developed a heuristic relational model that is still in use today. The so-called Johari Window (get it... Joseph and Harry) is an elegantly simple model that represents the changes in both self-awareness and group-awareness as relationships progress over time. The model is basically a square that is divided into four quadrants, each representing the different awareness levels of an individual versus the awareness levels of others around him or her.

The Johari Window

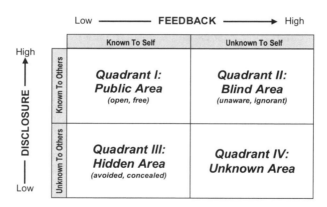

- **Quadrant I:** This is the area of free activity or public area. It refers to the behavior and motivation within a relationship that is known both by us as individuals and by others in the relationship.

- **Quadrant II:** This is the blind area where others can see things in ourselves that we are simply unaware of.

- **Quadrant III:** This is the avoided or hidden area. It represents things we know but do not reveal to others, (e.g., a hidden agenda, or matters about which we have sensitive feelings).

- **Quadrant IV:** This is the area of unknown activity in which neither we nor others are aware of certain behaviors or motives. Yet, it is assumed that these motives and behaviors exist because eventually some of them are discovered as influencing the relationship all along.

Now the interesting thing about the Johari Window is that it is actually dynamic and will change with relationships as they evolve. For instance, let's say you are given a new work assignment on the job and you are partnered with someone just recently hired into your organization. You have never worked with this person before but, because of the nature of the work you are doing, you are going to be working closely with him or her for quite some time.

At first, your Johari Relational Window might look like this…

The Johari Window: New Relationship

Low ———— **FEEDBACK** ————→ High

	Known To Self	Unknown To Self
High Known To Others	**Quadrant I:** **Public Area** *(open, free)*	**Quadrant II:** **Blind Area** *(unaware, ignorant)*
Unknown To Others **Low**	**Quadrant III:** **Hidden Area** *(avoided, concealed)*	**Quadrant IV:** **Unknown Area**

(vertical axis: DISCLOSURE — High to Low)

Basically, because you don't know one another very well, Quadrant I will be smaller because you have yet to share much free/public information with one another. The level of open awareness in the relationship is limited. As time moves on, the model might shift as such.

The Johari Window: Relationship Over Time

Low ———— **FEEDBACK** ————→ High

	Known To Self	Unknown To Self
High Known To Others	**Quadrant I:** **Public Area** *(open, free)*	**Quadrant II:** **Blind Area** *(unaware, ignorant)*
Unknown To Others **Low**	**Quadrant III:** **Hidden Area** *(avoided, concealed)*	**Quadrant IV:** **Unknown Area**

(vertical axis: DISCLOSURE — High to Low)

Quadrant I becomes larger as more of the reasons behind motivation and behavior are revealed and shared (i.e., you become more knowing and open with one another). As you can imagine, the best and more productive relationships would be the ones where, through open communication and sharing, Quadrants II, III, and IV were able to shrink due to the growing of Quadrant I. In other words, we stop hiding things in the relationship (Quadrant II), keep learning about ourselves through the relationship (Quadrant III) and continue discovering as part of the relationship (Quadrant IV) so that both we and the other individual(s) are more out in the open about the nature and direction of the relationship. This applies to any relationship, be it working with a new person at work, dating someone for the first time, or building a new organization.

Now, when it comes to working to build a more open, aware relationship in terms of the Johari Window, there are some interesting rules to keep in mind.

- A change in any one quadrant will affect all other quadrants.
- The smaller the first quadrant, the poorer the communication.
- Threat tends to decrease awareness; mutual trust tends to increase awareness.
- It takes energy to hide, deny, or to be blind to behavior that is involved in interaction.
- Forced awareness (exposure) is undesirable and usually ineffective.

Let's take a moment to focus on that last bullet point because it has a huge impact on our willingness to become more self-aware. In any relationship, if you are being confronted with something you either did not know about yourself (Quadrant III) or something you thought you had hidden from others (Quadrant II), how would you react? Many of us would immediately go into defensive mode. Similarly, if you were revealing something that had been hidden or denied from the group and you just "dropped a bomb" on them, what would their reaction be? How would it impact the relationship as a whole?

We keep things hidden or blocked from ourselves and others for a reason. Being confronted abruptly on these issues, can have a major backlash. Unfortunately, this type of confrontational awareness is often used within relationships. The trick is to move from confrontational awareness to self-awareness.

Confrontational Awareness Versus Self-Awareness

A few years ago, one of the authors (Dick Huseman) was making a presentation at a coaching conference in London. At the end of his talk, he was about to make the usual dash to the airport when he noticed Tim Gallwey (author of the **Inner Game of Tennis**) was speaking later that day. He made the decision to change his flight and stay and hear Mr. Gallwey speak.

At first, he was disappointed in his decision to stay as much of the early part of the presentation was Tim playing a black and white video that was over 30 years old. The tape showed Tim attempting to teach a rather hefty woman in a muumuu how to play tennis. The woman maintained that she had never been on a tennis court. That part was easy to believe as you watched her first attempts to hit the ball. Laughter started to break out in the audience.

Tim then provided a suggestion... "When the ball hits the court, say, 'Bounce!' and when your racket strikes the ball, say, 'Hit!'" As she implemented the "Bounce/Hit" technique, slowly but surely, she was able to return several forehand shots. Next, she could keep her backhand shots in play. Tim explained that the Bounce/Hit concept created self-awareness that connected the mind to what the body was doing. He continued to give the woman other suggestions for creating self-awareness as she continued to practice. Finally, she could serve.

Here is the unbelievable part – she was able to do all of this playing in her muumuu, using a racket she had never held in her hand before, in about 20 minutes time!

Tim Gallwey ended his presentation by stating – "It is only through self-awareness that people take ownership for what they do and what happens to them."

Break**OUT**

There are actually two types of awareness – self-awareness and confrontational awareness. Confrontational awareness is the insight gained by an individual when presented with outside data regarding his or her strengths, weakness or traits. In organizations, this type of awareness is often collected and disseminated in the form of a 360-degree survey or other feedback device. This is a form of feedback that generally fosters confrontational awareness. It offers feedback in the format of, "Here is how other people score you." The problem with confrontational awareness is that often there is a disassociation between the feedback offered and the individual's self-perception of their own performance. Feelings of defensiveness or denial can block true acknowledgement and acceptance of the feedback provided.

Self-awareness, on the other hand, goes one step further. Here, an individual internalizes feedback and accepts its validity within his or her own mental and emotional processes. In other words, they "get it." They see, in and of themselves, how their personality, mindset, and behavior resulted in the feedback reflected by others.

Sometimes, we have to start with confrontational awareness simply because it is the only way to get past our PCC's. But this must be done with care. Remember back to our list of Johari Window considerations, "Threat tends to decrease awareness." Often, when confronted with new or different feedback, we come away feeling judged or put down… with everyone pointing out our weaknesses.

In terms of building your own self-awareness or helping others build theirs, recognize it is natural to feel defensive to ideas, perceptions and suggestions that go against how we see ourselves. But, also recognize that confrontational awareness can be a tool to get past some of our PCC's... helping us BreakOUT of our PCC hoosegow and reach new levels of self-awareness.

Prison or PRISM: A Matter of Rewiring

In 1666, Sir Isaac Newton described how by utilizing a prism, he was able to refract white light into its color elements and then re-constitute the colors back into white light. In terms of self-discovery, we need to do the same thing. We need to look at the different parts of ourselves and how they interact with each other to understand why and how we do the things we do.

There are many different "prisms" (i.e., self-discovery or analysis tools) for you to work with. As we mentioned before, you can use anything from meditation to mentors – whatever works for you. In fact we encourage you to use as many tools as you can to "see" the different parts of yourself.

It is interesting that one of the many uses of the optical prism is in submarine periscopes. A periscope uses two or more prisms to generate an image inside the windowless boat of what the outside world looks like. So, too, can the different prism-like self analysis tools help us see things beyond our limited views from within the depths of our lives.

Through them, we start to locate and target our PCC's. But, what then? As you discover different traits, characteristics and patterns in your life, what do you do? You start to rewire yourself... rewire how you think about things and how things cause you to act and react. Again, there are more tools and techniques available to you to rewire your mind than we can cover in the scope of this book. We recommend you go online or to your library and you will quickly discover hundreds of ways to help you rewire your mind.

However, we do want to point out one very interesting thing. Once you have discovered a PCC – once you have found it in the hidden recesses of your mind and shined a spotlight on it – an interesting thing happens. You automatically break your commitment to the PCC. The "commitment" aspect of premature cognitive commitment is nullified by your awareness of it and you become empowered with choice.

They say the best way to avoid a trap is to know it is there. Well, once you know a PCC exists, your mind is equipped to naturally rewire itself to no longer come to a conclusion without you... you are given back control over how you choose to think or act in response to a particular situation or event. You are given a choice to either stay in prison or generate a PRISM.

> ### *PRISM*
> *Positive Rewiring Instills Successful Mindsets*

Positive rewiring instills successful mindsets. This little acronym is a powerful reminder of the true purpose of self-discovery: taking control and having the power to make choices. But, in terms of BreakOUT, we have to make sure we make positive choices in order to be successful. We have to make sure we don't get stuck in the negative and really push the positive.

Arm Yourself With Your Strengths

It is an unfortunate reality that it is sometimes easier to focus on the negative things in our lives than the positive. When most of us get right down to it, we spend far more time worrying about the bad things ("where could things go wrong," "what if I don't get what I want," "I don't know if I can do it"), than on the good things ("look how far I've gotten already," "I know I can do this," "I believe in myself").

The true gift of self-awareness is not in discovering our weaknesses, but in discovering our strengths. Self-awareness provides you with an arsenal of things you do well. Knowing what you do well, how you like to handle things and tapping into your natural style gives you the edge in any situation or relationship. You don't just have to react blindly… you take what you are good at and leverage it appropriately for the situation you are in.

We all have things we are good at and things we aren't. Rather like trying to teach a rabbit to fly, so many of us spend all of our effort and energy working to do the impossible… take all the "bad" stuff in our lives and somehow miraculously turn it all into roses. Consider the following story.

Once upon a time, several animals in a forest decided to open a school. The "students" included a fish, an eagle, a squirrel, and a rabbit. They established a curriculum that included running, swimming, tree climbing, jumping and flying – all of the things that would help them become well-rounded animals.

On the first day of school, the rabbit went to the running class, where he was a star. He happily ran up the hill and down again to easily win the race. The rabbit thought to himself, "I can't believe it! School is great! I get to come here every day and do what I do best!"

The instructor said, "Rabbit, you have a great talent for running. You have great muscles in your rear legs and, with some training, you'll get even better."

The rabbit replied, "I love school! I get to do what I do best and I get to learn how to do it even better."

His second class was swimming. As soon as the rabbit saw the pool and smelled the chlorine, he said, "I'm not so sure about this class. Rabbits don't like to swim."

The instructor said, "You may not like it now, but years from now, you'll look back and think it was a good thing you learned to swim."

The rabbit's third class was tree climbing. The rabbit tried several times, but he always fell back to the ground. He did just fine in jumping class, but in his last class – the flying class – he had a real problem. He couldn't stay in the air. The teacher then made him take a psychological test and discovered he needed to be in remedial flying. In remedial flying, the rabbit had to practice jumping off a cliff. The teacher told him, "If you work hard enough, you can succeed."

On the second day of school, the swimming instructor announced, "Today, we jump in the water!"

The rabbit responded, "My parents don't swim, my brothers and sisters don't swim. No other rabbits I know swim. Rabbits don't even like to get wet. I want to drop the course."

The instructor replied, "You can't drop it. Drop/add is over. You either jump in or fail the course."

The rabbit jumped in and panicked. He went down once. He went down twice. Bubbles came up. The instructor saw he was drowning and pulled him up. The other animals had never seen anything quite as ridiculous as the wet rabbit. They chirped, they hissed, and they laughed at the rabbit. He was more humiliated than he had ever been in his life. He couldn't wait for class to be over that day.

When he went home, he hoped his parents would understand when he said, "I don't like school! I just want to be free to run and jump and not have to do all of the other things we have to do in school."

But his parents said, "If you are going to get ahead as a rabbit, you have to graduate."

"I don't want to graduate," cried the rabbit.

His parents replied, "You are going to graduate whether you like it or not."

The next day, he hopped slowly to school. He remembered that the principal had said that if any of the students ever had a problem, they could always come and talk to him. So, the rabbit went to the principal's office and told him, "I don't like school."

The principal said, "Really! Tell me why."

When the rabbit was through telling his tale, the principal said, "Rabbit, I hear you. I hear you saying you don't like school because you don't like swimming or flying. I think I have diagnosed the problem. I'll tell you what we'll do. You are doing really well in running and jumping. I don't think you need to work on those anymore. What you need to work on is swimming and flying. So, from now on, instead of taking running and jumping every day, you will take two classes each in both swimming and flying."

The rabbit heard this and got sick to his stomach. As he hopped out of the principal's office, he ran into his old friend, the Wise Old Owl. The Old Owl asked, "Why so glum, rabbit?"

The rabbit told the owl what had happened. The Owl replied, "Rabbit, life doesn't have to be this way. We could have schools and businesses where people are allowed to concentrate on what they do best, not what they do worst."

The rabbit was inspired. He promised himself that once he graduated, he would develop his own school where rabbits ran, fish swam, squirrels climbed trees, and birds flew. As he walked down the hall that day he thought to himself, "Now, wouldn't that be a great place to be?"

This story is not to say that we should only do the things we already do well. Of course, we can always improve ourselves... but doesn't it make far more sense to really power up those things that we are already good at than exhaust ourselves trying to get our "below average" stuff just up to "average?"

That is the true value of self-awareness leading to BreakOUT... stop the cycle of blindly reacting to life and taking the best that you've got to really make your life the best it can be.

> *Bugs may be perfectly happy without awareness, but after all, they restrict themselves to crawling under rocks.*

We In The Human Equation

The first part of this book talked about how we, as individuals, can help break through our own limitations to achieve the BreakOUTs we want in life. Hopefully, you've had a chance to take a good look at yourself and have become more aware of yourself and some of your own particular PCC's. Some of this awareness might have seemed familiar, some understandable, others aspects totally alien. But, all of these offer "in" sight to help you figure out where you are and help you get to where you want to be.

It's time to shift perspective a bit. The fact is that while we each have our own unique penchants for PCC's, there are several commonalities in how (and why) homo sapiens do the things they do.

To say that humans are a "logical" race is relatively inane. Now, we are capable of strong reasoning and logic. Indeed, it is a concept many are fascinated by... the pristine perfection of the mathematical universe or the fascination of thinking like Mr. Spock. But, we aren't robots and when it comes right down to it, there is an equally if not more fascinating study of the "human equation." It is this human equation that really tends to make things interesting and unpredictable when it comes to dealing with people.

People can be frustrating, irritating, incomprehensible, galling, grating, inflaming, exasperating, infuriating, provoking, maddening and annoying creatures to deal with. If you have ever been in a situation where you are trying to work in a group, isn't it amazing how there is always someone (maybe more than one) who just seems to want to muck everything up? Don't they realize that things should be done your way? They must have some really major PCC's if they can't see simple reason, right?

Okay, pot! You've called the kettle black. Now it's time to understand that all is not lost here. People do work together. They have united time and time again to reach once incalculable heights. Call it what you will... progress, evolution, reaching for the stars, whatever… people have worked together to get "it" done. Humans as a race, for good or bad, have broken out all over the place.

It is a fact that we can work together with people and use that combined people-power to help each of us get what we want. And, there are things that you can learn and implement that will help you in your interactions and relationships with others to maximize this people power (or human capital). There are patterns to human behavior. There are things that you can learn and put into practice that will help you lead others toward BreakOUT. These next three chapters will show you exactly how to do that.

Part II:

BREAKOUT
Understanding Human Behavior
As Your Key Out of Prison

BreakOUT

Chapter 4
Balancing The Equity Equation
(Why We Do What We Do)

Let's play a little role-playing game. You work for a company and you think that the company you work for doesn't value you or what you do… not really (if this seems like a familiar role for you, we're sorry). Given the rules of this game, how hard are you going to work every day? Do you give your 100 percent best effort or do you work only as hard as you need to so that you don't get fired? Do you do just enough to get by?

Why would any of us put in any extra effort, energy or initiative at work when we feel that the company might sacrifice us without another thought if the balance sheet needed a boost? When employees have this attitude, then companies get the bare minimum effort of what they need. They don't even come close to getting the effort they want.

Doing More Because You Want To

There is a term: discretionary effort. Discretionary effort isn't necessarily about working more hours or taking on more responsibilities or jobs. Discretionary effort is what happens when people throw themselves into a job with their head and their heart, voluntarily giving their full attention, focus and creativity toward the attainment of company goals. It's the enthusiasm and drive we've all applied at some time in our life, whether we were playing a favorite sport, working on a pet project or were aiming at winning a prize we very much wanted. At those times, every fiber in our being was focused on achieving our goal – not because we had to, but because we deeply, passionately, wanted to.

Discretionary /dis-'kre-sh&n-ary/

1 a : ability to make responsible decisions **b :** individual choice or judgment **c :** power of free decision or latitude of choice

Effort /'e-f&rt/

1 a : conscious exertion of power: hard work **b :** a serious attempt **c :** the total work done to achieve a particular end

For the most part, leaders miss the boat on this. They rarely know how to tap into this drive and passion. If they did, they could inspire superior performance, make their people happier and more secure, and their customers would be more than satisfied. It is discretionary effort that can guarantee the high performance levels that will beat out the competition and get your team to meet even its most far-reaching goals.

But again, who is willing to give their discretionary effort in a game where shareholders are positioned as kings and queens while employees are viewed as mere pawns? You have to *give* to *get*. How? By understanding how you impact what people do (and don't) do.

Human Performance
(Mandatory Effort Vs. Discretionary Effort)

© 1998, Richard C. Huseman, Ph.D.

Oh, Behave!

In business today, most leaders do something called "managing for results." Let's say a leader wants a 15 percent sales increase by the end of next quarter. The leader focused solely on results would be fixated on the number of units sold each week. But a leader looking to manage behavior, on the other hand, wouldn't really focus on the units, he or she would be focusing strongly on what behaviors were needed on the part of their people to produce the units needed to reach the 15 percent increase – and what they as leaders could do to positively impact those behaviors.

The main issue for leaders is how to focus on the specific key behaviors that will lead to the high performance needed to guarantee success. That is what the rest of this chapter is all about.

Why We Do The Things We Do

In the days before heightened airport security, we were waiting in line one day at an airport curbside for our bags to be checked. We engaged in the popular "waiting in line" sport of watching what the people at the front of the line were doing. Most of them would hand the skycap a few dollars and ask him to make sure their bags got on the right plane.

The person directly in front of us, however, took an entirely different approach. He didn't offer the skycap a tip, but he did sternly lecture the skycap about taking special care of his two bags. He swore loudly when one of his bags tipped over accidentally, then angrily stalked off toward his gate. As we stepped up to take our turn, the skycap's broad smile caught our attention.

"I don't understand," I told him. "How are you able to keep smiling when you sometimes have to deal with such difficult people?"

"What do you mean?" he asked.

"That fellow who just swore at you," I replied.

The skycap smiled again. "Oh, that dude? People like him are easy. You see, he's heading for L.A., but his bags are going to Detroit!"

You see, there are these two things called equity and reciprocity. Equity and reciprocity work together to explain that when people don't feel that they are getting their fair share, they'll get even.

Let's start with equity. People **give** to **get**. Seems pretty simple, doesn't it? You work at your job and expect to get paid. You put change in a vending machine and expect to get your gum. You hug your significant other when they walk in the door at home and expect to get hugged back. You give to get.

Now, what happens if you give and don't get what you want or expect back? Well, at work you might mumble (if only to yourself), "I don't get PAID enough to put up with this!" The vending machine might get a kick – your significant other might, too. But what it boils down to is that when we give and then don't get, we feel shortchanged and act out. That's reciprocity.

What can be extracted from notions of equity and reciprocity is that what we give in balance to what we get determines our behavior. If we get what we expect and want, we'll keep giving in the same way. If we don't get what we want or expect, we stop or change what we are giving. This is the basis for the **Equity Equation**.

The Equity Equation has a rich history in philosophy, economics, anthropology, and psychology. In fact, the notion of equity was first set forth more than two thousand years ago. In his *Nicomachean Ethics*, Aristotle left little doubt that what people give and get is at the core of human relationships.

> *The very existence of the state depends on reciprocity...It is exchange that binds men together.*
> *– Aristotle*

Nothing in the "give to get" principle Aristotle set forward over 20 centuries ago has changed. Consider our skycap. Whether he knew it or not, he was reacting to an imbalance in his Equity Equation. When faced with a guy who was rude, condescending and who didn't even offer him a tip, the skycap "evened the equity score" by making sure the man's bags didn't get to the correct destination.

As leaders, while we might smile at the skycap's story, we need to consider the fact that we probably have no idea when or how often our people have been sending our bags to the wrong destination.

It is the Equity Equation and the relationship between give to get that is at the heart of human behavior – both at home and at work.

> *If you give enough people what they want,*
> *eventually, you will get what you want.*
>
> *– Anonymous*

The Give To Get In Relationships

As leaders, we want employees to be productive and committed. But we are often disappointed when they arrive late for work, take extended breaks and lunch hours, and call in sick even though we're sure that they're not. We wonder why they sometimes pad their expense accounts, work on personal projects during work hours, take company property home for their personal use, and even commit acts of sabotage. And we feel especially betrayed when they suddenly quit their jobs and go to work for another company – especially when it is our major competitor.

But, hold on. Before leaders, including you, start blaming the people working for their lack of loyalty, you might first want to try looking in the mirror. Remember, people give to get. So, if you aren't getting what you need from a relationship, then chances are you're not giving either– at least not the right things.

Let's try a short exercise. Think about one important work relationship you have – with a subordinate, co-worker, boss, spouse, child, friend, etc.

On the left-hand side of the work area on the next page, draw up a list of all the contributions you make to this relationship – what you are giving. If it's with your employees, you might be providing them with pay, job security, professional development opportunities, etc.

What I Give	What I Get

Make your list as lengthy as you can. Notice that this list is titled "What I Give."

On the right-hand side of the work area, make a second list of "What I Get." Write down all the benefits that you are receiving from your relationship. Loyalty? Support? Hard work? Creativity? Talent? Make this lengthy, too, if you can.

No item is too big or too small. For both lists, do not – repeat, do not – number the items. Just list them.

Now sit back and compare your two lists. Don't count the number of items on each one. Some things are more important than others. And you've probably left some items off both lists. Instead, answer this simple question:

Considering all that you give to your relationship versus all that you're getting from it, who is getting the better deal?

Choose one from the following three options:

❑ I'm getting the better deal.

❑ We're getting an equally good deal.

❑ The other person is getting a better deal.

Now, let's consider your answer in terms of the three Laws of
Equity.

Equity Law I: People Give To Get

> *People evaluate their relationships by*
> *comparing what they give to a relationship*
> *with what they get from it.*

What you contribute to relationships ("What I Give") we call
Inputs. What you receive in return ("What I Get") we call
Outcomes. Moments ago when you compared what you gave
to your work relationship and what you got from it, you were
evaluating your Inputs versus your Outcomes. You made a
conscious attempt to calculate your give to get ratio for this
particular relationship. The fact is, most of the time, probably
without even realizing it, you have made similar comparisons
subconsciously. And not just with this specific relationship.
You are processing your Equity Equation in all relationships,
all the time.

Picture a tiny computer-like gizmo in the back of your mind.
This computer tracks what you put into relationships and what
you get back. This computer switches on when you first pop
into the world, and it shuts down only when you close your
eyes for the last time. You can't turn it off. It keeps on going,
categorizing new Inputs and Outcomes, reprioritizing their
importance, and sometimes removing them completely. All the

time this computer is functioning, it's calculating and recalculating your **Equity Score**.

Usually this computer gizmo is humming along so quietly you don't even know it's operating. But if Inputs and Outcomes get too far out of balance, then it will let you know in a hurry that your Equity Score is too lopsided one way or another.

So, what's your Equity Score for the relationship you were just thinking about? If your answer was, "I'm getting the better deal," then you may be Over-Rewarded in this relationship.

If your answer was, "We are getting an equally good deal," then your Inputs are fairly equal to your Outcomes and your Equity Equation is in balance.

But, if your answer was, "The other person is getting a better deal," then you may be Under-Rewarded (you aren't getting enough from the relationship because your Inputs are getting too far ahead of your Outcomes).

In the case of workers in the United States, a good percentage of them really feel under-rewarded. How do we know? During the last few years, we've asked several thousand people, both managers and hourly workers, in some of America's largest corporations to tell us who's getting the better deal – they or the organization they work for. The chart below lists the troubling results.

Who Has Equity in the Workplace

	Managers	Non-Managers
Feel over-rewarded	13%	7%
Feel equitably rewarded	34%	10%
Feel under-rewarded	53%	83%

As you can see, over half of the managers in the organizations we surveyed feel Under-Rewarded (they think their organization is getting the better deal). What's perhaps even more troubling is that more than 80 percent of non-managers feel that their employer is getting the better deal.

Psychologists don't know how people make the actual comparison between what they give and what they get from relationships. Some psychologists think we compare ourselves to someone in a position or situation similar to our own.

For example, someone might feel underpaid for the amount of work done because a coworker does less work but gets paid the same salary. Or someone might feel Under-Rewarded if they are passed over for promotion and someone else who has fewer years experience with the company receives the position instead.

Others think people compare their Inputs and Outcomes against a standard that experiences earlier in life have etched into their mind. For example, people who have been married more than once might gauge Inputs and Outcomes in their current marriage by what they gave (or didn't give) and got (or didn't get) in their previous marriage(s).

A third possibility is that people compare their Inputs and Outcomes to what the other person in the relationship seems to be giving and getting. So, you yourself might feel you're getting the better deal if the other person is putting more time and effort into your relationship, but you're giving that person a lot less in return.

All of which leads us to Equity Law II.

Equity Law II: Inequity Creates Stress

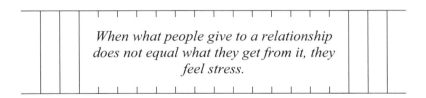

When what people give to a relationship does not equal what they get from it, they feel stress.

While nobody seems to know the basis for how people make comparisons between Inputs and Outcomes, it's clear that people do make these comparisons. These calculations produce one of three feelings:

- **Over-Rewarded:** Getting more than they're giving

- **Equitably Rewarded:** Getting as good as they're giving

- **Under-Rewarded:** Getting less than they're giving

But it's not just how people *feel* about these relationships, it's how they *react* to those feelings. The stress you feel over inequitable relationships – yes, even the ones where you've got the better deal – depends on who feels they're being cheated. People who are getting more than they're giving tend to feel *guilt*. People who are giving more than they're getting often experience *resentment*.

The Guilt of Over-Reward

Have you ever received too much change after a purchase in a department store, but you didn't realize it until you were in the car? Have you received a lavish gift from a friend for whom you did a very small favor? If so, then you know how it feels to be Over-Rewarded.

Two university professors once shared what has become our favorite example of Over-Reward. Several years ago, as part of a research project, the professors sent out holiday greeting cards to 528 total strangers. More than one hundred of their surprised recipients of the holiday greeting responded with either a card of their own, or an entire letter.

While most of the returning cards contained only a signature, many others included handwritten notes about their family or recalling old friendships with these two professors. Some people even included pictures of their families, pets, and friends. Only six people who sent back cards said that they couldn't remember the professors and asked for more information!

The reason the professors got so many responses is that people do try to keep relationships balanced evenly, and the guilt of being Over-Rewarded causes some people to respond in unexpected ways.

The Resentment of Under-Reward

The way people respond to feeling guilty about being Over-Rewarded can be odd, even funny. But it's the flip side of the give to get stress spectrum leaders have to worry about. When people feel the resentment of being Under-Rewarded, watch out!

Remember that 53 percent of managers and 83 percent of non-managers feel Under-Rewarded in their relationships with their organizations. Some people are probably only mildly irritated by this situation. Others are genuinely angry. When people are frustrated and angry because they are giving more than they are getting, that feeling compels them to react predictably, decisively, and, often, destructively.

This leads us to the final Equity Law.

Equity Law III: People Will Attempt To Restore Equity

> *People who feel stress in relationships*
> *because they give more than they get will*
> *engage in behaviors to restore equity.*

Remember the expression we have all mumbled (or shouted) at one time or another, "I'm not *PAID* enough for this!" This utterance says, "I'm not getting the Outputs I need from our work relationship" and is a huge warning sign that an employee feels badly Under-Rewarded. When people feel the resentment of being Under-Rewarded, they will try to restore the balance of equity in one of three ways.

1. People Will Reduce Inputs

2. People Will Increase Outcomes

3. People Will End The Relationship

1. People Will Reduce Inputs

Think about a relationship in which you experienced the frustration of Under-Reward. Did you try and even the score by giving less to the relationship? Probably. In organizations,

Under-Rewarded people will most certainly find ways to even the score. How? They will:

At Work

Come to work later

Do less work

Do careless work

Call in sick

Take extended breaks and lunch hours

"Forget" to carry out instructions

At Home

Come home late

Neglect chores or responsibilities

Give the silent treatment

Cancel scheduled dates

Not return phone calls

Stop sharing the covers

And, as we all know, there have been several tragic cases where people have felt so Under-Rewarded that they have resorted to violence… against their bosses and coworkers… or against family members or loved ones.

People have very little trouble figuring out how to restore equity in work relationships. An executive once told us about his resentment at being passed over for an important promotion. He decided to find another job. But while he was looking for that job, he simply sat around his office, doing as little as possible. He says that he felt a certain sense of satisfaction when he finally resigned three months later, because in some small way he had evened the score.

Another person described his high school summer job working in a peach packing shed. His job was to top off each basket with the best looking peaches from off a conveyor belt. Doing so would mean that peach buyers who opened the baskets to inspect them would think that each basket contained only the finest peaches.

One night, when he and two coworkers were angered by having to work until midnight four shifts in a row, the three of them began topping off randomly chosen baskets with small, bruised, and even rotten peaches. Although he feels guilty today about engaging in this act of sabotage, at the time, he and his coworkers felt enormous satisfaction at the owner's embarrassment when buyers claimed that the company was trying to sell bad peaches.

2. People Will Increase Outcomes

People who feel Under-Rewarded can also try to even their Equity Score by trying to change their Outcomes from a relationship. People will ask for:

At Work

Pay raises

Promotions

Increased job security

Job transfers

Better working conditions

At Home

Nicer home/living conditions

More of the other person's time

Decrease amount of chores/responsibility

Special considerations or favors

Invite the in-laws to stay for a month

If they don't get what they ask for, employees might increase their Outcomes in other, more destructive ways:

At Work

Working on personal projects while at work

Padding expense accounts

Taking company property home

Stealing from company

Sabotage their own work and other people's, too

At Home

Cheat on spouse or lover

Misuse joint assets

Speak negatively about other to friends and coworkers

Boil pet rabbit

Maybe these actions don't really even the score, but, even so, they do let people feel they're doing something to restore equilibrium to the relationship.

In business, stealing is unfortunately one of the ways in which people try to restore equity, and it's a lot more widespread than most people think. Studies have found that nearly two-thirds of all fast-food restaurant robberies involve current or former employees! In addition, a 1999 National Food Service Security Council found that about half of all restaurant workers have admitted to stealing some form of cash, property or both – and those statistics do not include stealing food.

Stealing to restore equity happens farther up the corporate ladder as well. An executive recently told us how outraged she was when she discovered that one of her subordinates was being paid $2,300 more than she was. She immediately confronted her plant manager. He confirmed that she was indeed making less money than her subordinate.

"I wish I could do something about it, but the company simply has to pay more to get good people these days," he told her.

Several weeks later, she quit her job. As she was emptying her desk, she slipped a dictionary that belonged to her employer into her briefcase.

"I've never stolen anything in my life," she told us. "But for some reason I just picked it up and carried it out." As she passed through security, she was terrified that someone might want to check what was in her briefcase. No one did. And today that book gathers dust on a shelf in her study. She calls it "my $2,300 dictionary."

3. People Will End the Relationship

The third way that Under-Rewarded people restore equity is simply to end the relationship. Each day across this country hundreds of people quit their jobs, end their marriages or break off relationships with friends and family.

Obviously, "quitting" doesn't bring equity back to the relationship. But for some frustrated people, there appears to be no better option. The stress of being shortchanged in a very important relationship in their life finally drives them to break the relationship off completely. Usually, they've tried other means first to restore the balance, and those efforts have failed. They decided to leave before the inequity gets even worse.

And, in today's job market, choosing to quit might actually improve someone's situation considerably.

What the three Laws of Equity tell us is that people want equity in their relationships at work with their bosses, subordinates, coworkers, and organizations – just as they want the same kind of fairness at home with their significant others, children and friends. When they feel that the relationship is out of balance, they'll do everything in their power to restore that give to get equilibrium, even if they've got to end the relationship to do it.

Personal Reactions to Equity

Maybe you're troubled by the concept of people always expecting something in return for their contributions to a relationship. You might be saying to yourself, "That's not me. I give a lot, and I don't expect much in return."

During the past several years, we've discovered exceptions to the Equity Laws. In fact, we developed a little analytical tool we call the Equity Sensitivity Test. Having given this test to thousands of people, we can honestly say that some people, in fact, actually do want to give more than they get. We call these people **Benevolents**. Many others, though, prefer to get more than they give. We call them **Entitleds**. But most people do look for a balance between their Inputs and Outcomes – between what they give and what they get. We call people in this category **Equity Sensitives**.

Benevolents

This group is by far the smallest. They usually follow the old Calvinistic philosophy that it is "better to give than receive." They prefer that they give more than they get for several reasons. Some are altruistic people who simply want to do for others, no matter what the return might be. Still others give more than they get so they can feel good about themselves. Benevolents are the givers in relationships.

Entitleds

Entitleds are the getters in relationships. Some Entitleds are members of the "Me" generation – people who would get ahead without doing rather than get ahead by doing. Yet, many Entitleds are extremely talented and valuable players in the workplace. In some instances, it is not surprising that employees are taking more of an entitlement perspective in regard to their jobs. As a result of the loss of the old workplace contract, they see many corporations taking the position that "It's all about shareholder value… everything else is secondary." Is it any wonder that some employees have adopted a similar motto, "I have to take care of me first, and the company comes second?"

Equity Sensitives

Most of us, though, are Equity Sensitives. We try to keep a balance between what we give and what we get from our relationships. We take the temperature of our work and personal relationships by constantly gauging what we contribute to them and what we get in return.

In short, Equity is the most powerful motivation behind why people behave, perform and react the way that they do in relationships. The Equity Equation explains why people are unproductive, unsatisfied, uncommitted and unhappy at work and at home.

BreakOUT Equity

Knowing now that people (including you) give to get, what does this mean in terms of motivating someone to BreakOUT? The "get" would have to be pretty big, wouldn't it, to get us to change how we think and act? Remember those PCC's are tough customers and will resist change to a relatively strong degree.

Our first advice to you, BreakOUT leader, is to consider Outcomes that go beyond just traditional ones. In business, many leaders make the assumption (another term for PCC) that the only way to give more to people is to reward them financially in some way. It is one way to increase an Outcome... but consider some of these others in terms of work relationships.

- Accomplishment
- Meaningful Work

- Ability Utilization
- Achievement
- Challenge
- Job Security
- Recognition
- Promotion
- Personal Worth

Pay can be important, yes. But, there are many other things people get from work.

Remember the "What I Give/What I Get" list you filled out earlier in the chapter? Do all of the things you listed have the same value or importance to you? Probably not. For some people, recognition or accomplishment might be more important than pay. At home, spending quality time with a loved one or taking out the trash once in a while might be a better "give" than any expensive present.

Consider your relationships and what the people you work and live with want to "get"... and then give it to them to get the BreakOUT you want.

Dear leader, knowing why people do what they do is one of the biggest and best tools you have in your tool kit. When you are relating to people, one of your BreakOUTs can be really understanding why you and the people around you behave the way you do. Your next step can be knowing how and when best to apply this new understanding. It's time to re-learn your ABC's.

Chapter 5
The ABC's of Behavior
(Before And After)

The fact that people give to get explains why people do the things they do. The next step is how you, as a leader, can use this information to motivate and affect what it is people do… in other words, how you get them to "behave" in ways you want them to. All it takes is reviewing your ABC's.

The ABC Behavior Model, long used by behavioral psychologists, basically says that behavior is influenced by two factors: what comes before a behavior (the Antecedent) and what happens after the behavior (the Consequence). Together, the Antecedent and Consequence dynamic work together to affect all current and future behavior. Let's start by looking at Antecedents.

Antecedents

An antecedent is something that occurs prior to a behavior. Within an organization, these antecedents might include instructions, policies, procedures, training, performance goals, vision statements, etc. Antecedents set the stage for a behavior to occur. They do not, however, guarantee that a behavior will actually occur.

It's like getting ready for a play. You can stage the lighting, get all the props ready and have a beautiful set design... none of which matters if the play stinks.

People, especially managerial types, like antecedents a lot. Antecedents often provide the structure and/or foundation for a behavior. Examples include establishing goals, giving instructions, providing training, etc. We all know people (even the ones in the mirror) who love spending lots of time telling people exactly what to do, how to do it and under what conditions it must be done. These are our Antecedent fans.

In fact, studies have shown that the majority of leaders in organizations spend 80 percent of their time with the people they work with managing antecedents. But, according to the ABC model, these leaders are wasting much of their time. Antecedents only affect 20 percent of behavior. That means many leaders are putting 80 percent of their effort into trying to get their people to do what they want them to do and only getting a 20 percent result. If you are working to get a really big BreakOUT from your people, this equates to a huge waste of time and energy.

All of those policy/procedure manuals and detailed instructions do very little in terms of getting people to do what you want them to. It's what happens afterward that counts. We have to reverse our emphasis in terms of antecedents and consequences. Instead of focusing on telling people "how" to behave, it is far better to either reinforce or readjust behaviors after the fact through the use of consequences.

Consequences

If an antecedent is something that happens before a behavior, a consequence, not too surprisingly, is what happens after a behavior does or does not occur. Consequences can be either positive or negative.

- A positive consequence is when you reinforce a behavior (they did it right or they did well). The purpose of positive consequences is to motivate and inspire people to do more of the same behavior. Examples include a note of appreciation, pat on the back or reward of some kind.

- A negative consequence is when you criticize a behavior (they did it wrong or not at all). The purpose of negative consequences is to discourage people from doing something you don't want them to do again. Examples include everything from a gentle admonishment to a written warning.

Common sense tells us that positive consequences would be the preferred feedback form we would like to receive. It is a rare person who likes getting negative feedback on their behavior. Most of us like being told we have done well. Unfortunately, especially in the business world today, there is a severe shortage of positive feedback or consequence to support our good behavior. Many times, we work in environments where the motto is, "You are doing fine – if you're not, we'll definitely let you know in the most unpleasant way possible."

Why is this? Because the unfortunate truth is that most leaders simply don't know their ABC's. They spend most of their time managing antecedents and only focus on consequences after things have already gone wrong.

The ABC Behavior Model

Always remember it is the consequence side of the model that has by far the greatest impact on behavior – consequences drive 80 percent of behavior. Antecedents may jump-start the way people act, but consequences are what keep it going.

For example, consider cigarette smoking. For years, the federal government puzzled over whether cigarette packages should have a warning label on them, then took even longer figuring out what the warning should say. The first message went something like this: "Warning – The Surgeon General has determined that smoking *MAY BE* dangerous to your health" (emphasis added).

Not too surprisingly, very few smokers took the warning to heart and threw their unlit cigarettes into the trash. So, lawmakers tried again. This time they tried something more hard-hitting: "Warning – the Surgeon General has determined that cigarette smoking *IS* dangerous to your health" (emphasis added). Again, the public was not deterred from lighting up, even with the dramatic rewording of the warning (sarcasm added). The antecedent of putting a warning on cigarette packages had virtually no impact on whether people chose to smoke or not.

What has had an effect are other factors (consequences) which are a lot more direct: Hefty fines for people who smoke on planes and public outcry for those who light up in many public restaurants and buildings. The consequences of being hit directly in the pocketbook or the ego if they light up has curtailed far more smokers than any finger-wagging antecedents could have done.

Curtailing cigarette smoking is a lesson in psychology. No matter how enticing or intimidating an antecedent is, it's not going to have a long-lasting effect unless it's paired with a meaningful consequence. If we're in a huge rush, a sign that reads, "Reserved Parking" isn't likely to stop us from parking there, especially if we know we'll only be a minute. But, a sign which reads, "Danger – High Voltage" is much more likely to grab our attention. Why? Because we know that if we ignore that particular antecedent, the consequence could be literally quite shocking.

Consequences Really Do Determine Behavior

Every day, people leave work either more motivated or less motivated to come back the next day. What makes the difference? Whatever happened to them that day. Performance is about what happens every day. Each time we do something, something else happens as a result (i.e., a consequence). There are four types of these results: Extinction, Punishment, Negative Reinforcement and Positive Reinforcement.

Extinction: Not Getting What You Want

For example, perhaps you present a new idea to your boss. Even though you offer it several times, your boss seems either too busy or unwilling to listen to you. After a couple more tries, you throw up your hands and never mention the subject again.

Punishment: Getting Something You Don't Want

Suppose you miss a Monday morning meeting because you wrote the wrong date into your calendar and, as a result, you lose a potential client. From that point forward, you will definitely start to confirm your appointments for the following week on the preceding Friday.

Negative Reinforcement: Escaping/Avoiding Something You Don't Want

Even though you know you've got many more important things to do than take out the trash, you do it anyway. You know if you don't, your spouse or significant other will be all over your back the next day if the trash doesn't get picked up. So, to avoid this, you just go ahead and drag the can to the curb.

Positive Reinforcement: Getting Something You Want

Your boss offers to upgrade your computer. She has two reasons, she tells you. One is so getting your job done will be easier. Second, she tells you she wants her best player to be even more effective than you already are. As a result, your performance shoots up, not just because your equipment is now sportier but also because you just got a major ego boost.

Of these four categories, two (Positive and Negative Reinforcement), help increase performance. Two others (Punishment and Extinction), reduce performance. Many leaders work under the mistaken assumption that if people are performing well that there's no need to say anything. Bad idea. Doing nothing *is a consequence.* It means that no matter how good a job your people do, you won't reward them in any way. Soon they'll stop trying and performance will drop. So, not doing anything is actually a form of extinction.

You, as a leader, change the behavior of your people both by what you do *and* what you don't do. The consequences you do or do not provide are actually among the most important Outcomes (remember Equity Theory) people are seeking in their relationship with you.

Consequences and the Equity Equation

So, think back to the Equity Equation. Others are working hard to provide Inputs into their relationship with you. What you do or don't do about their hard work provides their Outcomes. In other words, you have a powerful opportunity to shape what people do and how well they do it. So, take a look at what you are doing to provide Consequences to people. Take the following Consequence Quiz:

The Consequence Quiz

1. What consequences am I providing to people after they have performed a behavior?

2. Are the consequences I am providing positive or negative?

3. Do I provide consequences right away or do I allow some time to pass after the behavior occurs to actually give them?

4. Do people know with any certainty what consequences to expect from me or do they wonder what (if any) consequences will be given?

First, if you could not think of any consequences you provide – you're in trouble. If you said that the consequences you give are:

☑ POSITIVE

☑ IMMEDIATE

☑ CERTAIN

then you're using consequences in a way that motivates people to do what you want them to do.   However, if your consequences are:

☑ NEGATIVE

☑ IN THE FUTURE

☑ UNCERTAIN

then you're shooting yourself in the foot.   You aren't encouraging people to act the way you want and, in fact, you may be encouraging them to act in ways you don't want. That means performance levels head south, and guess who looks bad as a result? (For the answer to this riddle, take a long, deep look in the mirror.)

The Role of Consequence History

You may be asking yourself if consequences come after a behavior, how can they possibly have an 80 percent impact on behavior? It's a bit like who came first, the chicken or the egg. Remember that we're all walking around with that equity calculator in our heads, keeping track of what we give and what we get and checking to see if the two balance out. That calculator is always on full alert to gauge the consequences that result from our behavior.

For example, suppose a minor issue at work has come up, and you decide to bring it to the attention of your boss. You go into her office and share your concern with her. Then she scowls and says, "The company doesn't react well to problems. Top management isn't really interested in your ideas. You need to focus on just doing your job."

You automatically log this conversation into your behavior calculator. Later, when an even bigger issue comes up, you'll look back in your history of consequences and decide that you're going to keep your mouth shut. The earlier consequence of having your boss slap you down for bringing a problem to her attention has transformed into an antecedent that discourages you from speaking up this time around.

Consequences get fed into our behavior calculator in two ways: directly and indirectly. Your boss telling you to mind your own business is an example of the direct path, when consequences become burned into our mind from our own personal experience. Most consequences, though, come to us indirectly. That's when you pick up on what you hear about other people's consequences. You don't have to try leaping out of a plane without a parachute to know that the consequences will be pretty unpleasant. And, many corporate cultures are rampant breeding grounds for indirect, negative consequences.

For example, suppose you and a coworker are in a two-hour meeting with one of the company's senior executives. The meeting is very productive. However, close to the end, your coworker and friend raises a problem he has with a decision made at a recent board meeting. The issue is a valid one, but your friend doesn't bring it up in the most tactful way. The senior executive loses his temper, cuts off your friend with a biting response, and ends the meeting abruptly.

Once the meeting is over, even though it was basically very productive, the one fact that gets communicated in rapid-fire fashion throughout the organization is how the senior executive lost his temper when he was asked a seemingly innocent and valid question. As a result, others throughout the organization decide to think twice before they raise any questions they might have with that particular executive. Why? Because their indirect consequence history *predicts* that the result could be a negative one, even though they have not witnessed the consequence first hand.

And don't think it stops there. The problem with associating a negative consequence with a particular behavior is that the association can spread. Let's say the temperamental executive we just described is actually a peer of yours and you hold similar titles in different divisions within the company. After hearing about how the other executive lost his cool during the meeting, your people might actually transfer that negative consequence to their relationship with you. They might decide not to ask questions about senior level decision-making because they think they, too, are going to be yelled at – even though you have never even raised your voice or become angry with anyone. You may have told your employees again and again that they can be open and direct in their communications with you and on several occasions, when they have asked you questions, you have tried to give very positive consequences to that behavior. However, one negative consequence – either acquired directly or indirectly – can cancel out many positive consequences in an individual's personal consequence history logbook.

As a leader, if your people are more likely to predict that their behaviors will result in a negative consequence rather than a positive one, they'll start to curb their behavior. In addition, their resistance will be very high when you try to get them to focus on any new behaviors for increasing performance or implementing some type of change (i.e., BreakOUT).

Now that we have discussed the role of equity in determining how people behave and the ABC's of how leaders influence behavior, there is one more type of BreakOUT that is needed. We have to fully appreciate the role relationships play within the scope of leadership.

What all this leads to is the basic reality that to influence, motivate, direct and lead people, you have to understand the subtle intricacies of how relationships develop over **time**. The time factor is the key to understating relationships... knowing that each and every interaction you have with someone impacts the whole of the relationship. You need to get smart in how you relate to others.

BREAKOUT

Chapter 6
Relational Intelligence
(Do You Know Your RQ?)

You've heard of IQ (how smart you are). You may have even heard of EQ (your emotional/social intelligence). But, have you heard of RQ (relational intelligence)? It is a person's RQ – more than any other factor – which differentiates an average leader from a truly exceptional one. Your understanding of RQ will play a major role in your effectiveness in unleashing the power of people.

Over the years, we have worked with thousands of leaders from almost every industry, both profit and non-profit, at all levels. The majority of these leaders (especially in the big, top floor offices) are highly intelligent... but being smart has not always guaranteed their success. In a study based on a national databank of 60,000 executives, having high levels of intelligence was found to play no significant role in determining a leader's effectiveness on the job. Indeed, many highly intelligent individuals have derailed as leaders. Why?

Well, some say it is because they lack EQ (emotional intelligence). In the decade of the 1990's, much has been said and written about a leader's emotional intelligence and how emotions and intuition play a critical role in a leader's success (or failure). EQ also emphasizes a leader's ability to "connect" with those they are trying to lead or influence.

In reality, leadership requires using both the head (IQ) and the heart (EQ). However, neither IQ nor EQ in and of themselves can guarantee your success as a leader. Make no mistake, they are both necessary. However, the value of IQ and EQ can only be truly realized when they are utilized in the framework of a person's RQ – Relational Intelligence.

Relating To People

RQ isn't about any specific trait or competency a leader needs to have to be effective. It is about the *relationship*, over time, between the leader and those the leader wants to influence and motivate. It is only within the critical context of the ongoing *relationship* that you as a leader can make the most of both your IQ and EQ.

To some extent, business has acknowledged the value of building and maintaining relationships, but most of these approaches focus on relationships with customers: relationship banking, relationship marketing, etc. What has received far less attention is a focus on the relationships leaders can forge with their employees, with other leaders and anyone else directly tied to their success. It is within a relational approach that truly great leadership can manifest itself.

What is Relational Intelligence (RQ)?

Relational intelligence (RQ) is a leader's ability to accurately perceive and utilize the dynamics of day-to-day interpersonal interactions with people and understand how these interactions impact the relationship over time. In other words, how what you do within a relationship today affects the relationship tomorrow.

On a micro level: A leader's IQ (head) and EQ (heart) do not operate independently or in a vacuum. Rather, IQ and EQ combine to play within the context of a relationship where the history of that relationship greatly impacts the behavior exhibited during any specific interaction within that relationship. Put simply, your relationship history with a person impacts any current interactions you have with that person. In turn, how you relate to a person today will impact your future interactions with that person. Thus, relational intelligence requires that you recognize that how you related to people in the past and how you relate to them today, will determine, to a large extent, the success or failure of how you relate to them in the future.

On a macro level: The relational dynamics that apply to one-on-one interactions become magnified when applied in the group setting of a team or organization. A leader's interactions with individual members of a group are combined and translated into a collective relational framework that becomes applicable across all members of the group. Thus, you not only maintain individual relationships with people, you also maintain a macro-level relationship with the entire group.

Conceptualizing Relational Intelligence (RQ)

Every relational interaction is actually 3-in-1. Within any one interaction, you must realize what factors are actually in play.

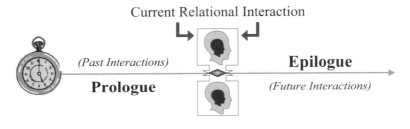

Current Relational Interaction

(Past Interactions)   **Epilogue**

Prologue   *(Future Interactions)*

The Ongoing Relationship

1. ***The Relational Prologue:*** the history of past interactions that have occurred in the relationship.

2. ***The Current Relational Interaction:*** the issues and dynamics at play within the context of the interaction at hand.

3. ***The Relational Epilogue:*** the impact that the current interaction, as well as all past interactions, will have on the relationship going forward.

When you are trying to unleash the power of people, your most important power is influence… not command and control. You must be aware that every interaction (both large and small) you have with your people either adds to or detracts from the influence you have in the ongoing relationship. However, it is during the more critical interactions where relational intelligence becomes most important. It's when there is a lot at stake that you might find yourself looking back on a relationship with a particular person and wish you had been "smarter" in how you handled the relationship in the past.

So, from the outset, you need to handle *every* interaction with people in terms of a long-term win/win scenario. One of the keys to relational intelligence is knowing that there are times when you will want to leave something on the "relationship table" to maintain the strength and vitality of the long-term ongoing relationship (i.e., you may need to compromise or give in a little on a less important issue so that when a big issue comes up, you've got some equity built up in the relationship).

Given the hectic pace of day-to-day, on-the-job interactions, leaders don't always take the time to think about RQ and what long-term effects their interactions might have on their team or individuals on the team. What can you do to be more RQ-smart?

Relational Intelligence (RQ): Getting Started

All of us have had the experience of laying awake at night re-living a particular interaction you had with someone that day that did not go well and wonder... why? Think of the prologue, current interaction, epilogue framework. Was there something from your past interactions with that person that could have affected what happened today? Did you handle things in keeping with the long-term relationship you want to build with this person or were you just going for the short-term win? These questions are what RQ is all about.

In addition, there are three other considerations that might help you leverage your RQ when interacting with people.

1. Be Aware Of Stamp Collecting

2. Use The Right Psychological Currency

3. Elevate Interactions To The Level Of Agreement

Let's take each one in turn and examine how being aware of these considerations can help you raise your RQ.

1. Be Aware Of Stamp Collecting: On occasion, you might find yourself in a situation where another person's reaction to a current interaction is far more volatile than the situation would appear to justify (i.e., they blow up for apparently no reason). These "blow-ups" aren't usually just about what is currently happening in the interaction but a result of some negative thing(s) that happened earlier in the relationship.

Maybe you're familiar with the trading stamps (Green Stamps) shoppers used to collect as a bonus for shopping in supermarkets and department stores. People pasted these stamps into little books, and when the books were filled, they could redeem them for toasters, clocks, even vacations. In relationships, we "collect" and "redeem" stamps as well, but usually the results aren't nearly as pleasant or productive.

An executive once told us about her "stamp" collection on a boss she once had early in her career. During the five years she worked for him, he did a lot of things to help her complete her stamp book. When they went out for lunch, he'd frequently be in the restroom when the check arrived. He would tell visitors to park in her parking place. He frequently took credit for her ideas and work. He made condescending remarks about women and insulted his own boss behind the boss' back. All during that time, the woman was mentally collecting her stamps of her boss' relational interactions with her.

Then, it was time to cash in the stamp book. A question arose about an expense report her boss had put in for payment. There was a mistake on the report claiming he had made a trip he had never taken. Now, her boss had always filled out and put in his own expense reports. However, when someone from accounting stopped in to check on it, her boss, in front of her, claimed she had made an error. The woman quit on the spot.

Her boss probably had no idea how many stamps he had accumulated in her relational stamp book. He probably thought she would just accept the blame without question. However, because of his considerable lack of RQ, he was completely unprepared when a "relatively" minor interaction resulted in her having collected the final stamp in her "relational stamp book" and triggered her to quit her job.

2. Use The Right Psychological Currency: With every interaction we have, we should work to build win/win relationships with people. However, we must take care that what we give to the relationship is actually something the other person wants.

How much is one dollar worth? A dollar will probably buy you the same ½ cup of coffee in California as it will in Florida. The exchange rate is the same on the East and West Coasts. When you travel to a foreign country, the exchange rate is usually fixed as well. One dollar will get you approximately 11 pesos, 5 francs, 104 yen, 5 rand and so on, depending on the exchange rate that day. In our economic transactions, the currencies are tangible and the rate of exchange is fixed.

In our relational interactions, we exchange "currencies" as well. But most of these relational currencies are not tangible and the exchange rate is rarely fixed.

In many instances, leaders have gone to great lengths to give something to the relationship that the other person doesn't really value (i.e., they offer them the wrong psychological currency). For example, if a person finishes a project ahead of schedule, you reward them with giving them more of the same type of work. The problem is, they hated that kind of work so much they did it early to get it out of the way.

In order to know what is actually valued and desired by the other individual in the relationship, you must be able to engage in clear and open communication. Sometimes, this will involve putting aside your agenda so that you can really listen to what the other person is trying to say. Take care not only to listen to the words being spoken, but also listen between the lines. In reality, only 7 percent of communication is language. The other 93 percent of communication is expressed non-verbally. So, use your RQ – be sure to listen to the *total* message being communicated, make sure you know what it is people want/need from their relationship with you and that they really know what you want/need from them. Then you know how you can pay them using the right psychological currency.

3. Elevate Interactions To The Level Of Agreement: When one of our relational interactions turns into a disagreement, the standard reaction is for both parties in the interaction to become defensive and start to argue about why "they" are right and the other person(s) are wrong. The more relationally intelligent approach to dealing with disagreement is to elevate the interaction back up to a level where everyone is in agreement (i.e., come back up to a point where everyone agrees and go from there). Then, from a point of agreement, the interaction can continue on to more specific issues.

For example, how many times have you been in a meeting where three different departments or divisions of your business were represented and they all had their own agendas and wanted different things. Most likely, the meeting quickly spiraled down into chaos where everyone closed themselves off to the group and only focused on what "they" wanted.

The next time this happens, you, as a relationally "smart" leader, should stop the downward spiral and get everyone clear on the fact that, though they may represent different departments or divisions, they are still on the same team – and they are all trying to win the game. From that perspective, the meeting could progress from a level of agreement with all parties focused on the same macro level goal. If the discussion began to spiral down again, it's up to you to go back up to the level of mutual agreement whenever you reach an apparent impasse with a person or group of people.

High RQ = Win/Win Relationships

Leadership really is a combination of IQ (the head) and EQ (the heart). But both IQ and EQ only reach their greatest potential when they are employed within a RQ framework (prologue, current interaction and epilogue).

Relational intelligence requires that instead of trying to get the most benefit out of every single interaction, you focus on the long-term benefits of your ongoing relationship... even if that means sacrificing an immediate benefit in order to maximize the relationship over the long-term. Exceptional leaders use their relational intelligence to make the most of all relationships, even ones where the only win/win scenario can only be found in ending the relationship. However, the primary focus for people with high RQ is to build and maintain long-term win/win relationships.

Obviously, for any leader trying to inspire BreakOUT from the people around him or her, RQ is absolutely essential. You won't ever be able to get someone to BreakOUT if you break them down first. And, so often, that's what ends up happening. Especially in today's hyper-competitive business world, it's the guy or gal up front who ends up crushing the people whose shoulders they are standing on. You may not want to admit it, but by taking on the title and role of leader, you've put yourself in the situation of both getting the fame… and taking the blame. There is only one thing that can save you… trust.

Trust: The Foundation Of Any Relationship

Trust, of course, is important in all relationships, but it's especially crucial between you and the people who you are trying to motivate and drive to BreakOUT. If you don't have it, you're going to get nowhere fast.

Several years ago, researchers at The Center for Creative Leadership identified the chief causes business executives fail in their organizations. At the very top of their list were arrogance and insensitivity to other people (RQ issues, here). Running a very close second was not being trustworthy.

Are you trustworthy? If you are like most people, based on a scale from 1 to 10 (10 being the most trustworthy), odds are that you consider yourself to be between a 7 or an 8. Now, using that same scale, as a whole, how trustworthy do you consider other people to be? The typical responses we hear to this question are 4, 5, or 6.

How does this relate to your job? A survey by researchers at Boston University found that 80 percent of employees in organizations simply don't trust top management.

Why? Well, let's start with some of your own biases. Assume that you believe that trustworthy people tell the truth and keep their word. Now make a mental list of occupations you see as being untrustworthy. How about used car salespersons? Mechanics? Politicians? Journalists? Lawyers? Given a little time, you probably could fill out a very long list. One reason we have trouble trusting others is our assumption is that they will take advantage of us, lie to us, cheat and steal from us, in order to get what they want from a relationship.

Another reason trusting others is difficult is that trust in relationships does not come about quickly. When beginning a new relationship, we tend to withhold trust until others prove that they can be trusted. People have to earn our trust just like they have to earn our respect and friendship. New employees are less likely to be given access to confidential company information than are senior employees who have already justified our confidence in them. Thus we refuse to trust other people who simply say, "Trust me." Our position is, "Show me first that you can be trusted!"

The final problem is that trust is very fragile, like a piece of fine china. Building a relationship based on trust can take a very long time, but smashing it can take only seconds. One simple violation of trust shatters whatever trust has been built, and we then suspect that the person can't be trusted at all, ever. Once our trust has been violated, we usually aren't willing to give that person a second chance. If we do, we do it very grudgingly.

So, how can you build and maintain trusting relationships with people? There are three essential qualities in any relationship on which trust is constructed:

- How competent people think you are.

- How caring people think you are about others.

- How dependable people think you are in being both caring and competent over time.

Building Trust

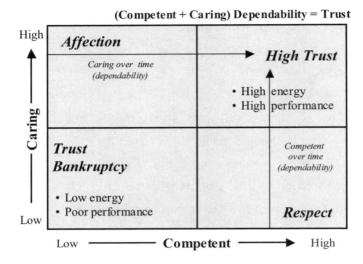

(Competent + Caring) Dependability = Trust

© 1998, Richard C. Huseman, Ph.D.

Depending on how people perceive your combination of competence and caring, you may find yourself in one of four types of trust relationships:

- Relationships based primarily on Respect

- Relationships based primarily on Affection

- Relationships in Trust Bankruptcy

- Relationships based on High Trust

Here is a guide to each one of these types of trust relationships.

Relationships Based On Respect

If people see you as being very competent at your job but caring little or not at all about people, you probably will earn the respect of those around you, but not their trust. Many of us have known people who are great at their jobs, but whose attitude toward people is so cold and indifferent that we would trust them only as far as we could throw them.

Relationships Based On Affection

If you are perceived as highly caring of others, but not perceived as very competent at what you do, those you work with may think of you affectionately as a friend or a kind person, but they won't necessarily think enough of your judgment to consider you much of a leader.

Relationships In Trust Bankruptcy

If the people who work with you don't see you as being either caring or competent (as many now see their organizations, thanks to the era of downsizing and merger), then your relationship with them is in trust bankruptcy. As a leader, your effectiveness in your relationships with the people who work with you is at great risk because there is simply no foundation on which to base the relationship.

Relationships Based On High Trust

If you are perceived by people to be both highly competent at your job and genuinely caring about people – and you are able to demonstrate these two qualities again and again over time (i.e., you are perceived as dependable), then you are well on your way to building high trust relationships with others. As a leader, high trust relationships are the foundation to fostering high performance relationships.

So, what's next, leader? You've learned why people do what they do (Equity's give to get). You understand you need to practice your ABC's (especially the C's) to get people to behave in ways you want them to. And, you've given your RQ a booster shot in terms of understanding how your relationships with people evolve over time.

What's missing to get you to affect BreakOUT for yourself and those you lead? You need to know how to get from A to B(reakOUT).

Chapter 7
BreakOUT Mapping
(It's A Trip)

Some of the best things you can do to help build human capital and lead people to BreakOUT aren't going to be written down for you in this book or anywhere else. You have to come up with them on your own. As a leader, you can't just follow the other guys around. You have to find your own way and then get those around you to follow *you*... you and not the other guy.

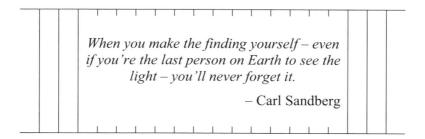

When you make the finding yourself – even if you're the last person on Earth to see the light – you'll never forget it.

– Carl Sandberg

Competitive Benchmarking

Over recent years, benchmarking has become extremely popular. If you aren't familiar with the term, benchmarking is the study of a competitor's product or business practices in order to improve the performance of one's own company. A good idea, right? By learning what the other guy is doing, and then doing the same things ourselves, we can beat them at their own game.

Wait… does that really sound right? Can anyone truly increase their competitive advantage by imitating the best practices of their competitors?

In terms of an analogy, let's go back to prison. Benchmarking in prison would mean that you would gather as much information as you could about the escape plans used by inmates who had successfully escaped from prisons like yours before. The trick is, their prison wasn't "exactly" like yours. It might have been similar in a few ways but very different in other ways. Are you likely to achieve a successful BreakOUT by following their plans and strategies to the letter? Is that really what BreakOUT means – doing what the other guys have done before? If you really were in a prison, focusing too much on a plan that was successful for someone else could be a disaster for you.

There is no question benchmarking can spark some ideas about different ways you could do things, but too often leaders and their organizations take this concept way too far. In our opinion, often far too much time, money and energy is dedicated to "researching and documenting" how the other guys do it.

Benchmarking Can Keep You On The Bench

First of all, how do you know their ideas are going to work with you? Like putting a square peg in a round hole, taking ideas from others and trying to force fit them to your organization's existing culture and structure can be a frustrating (and potentially fruitless) effort. You could put a whole lot of work into detailing a plan that really isn't right for you... but because benchmarking tells you it is a good way to go, you pursue that path anyway. As a result, your focus is taken away from other, more rewarding, possibilities. Benchmarking may get you a seat on the bench, but seldom will you play in the game at the same level of high performance of those you are trying to copy.

Plus, when organizations are benchmarking, they are rarely executing. While everyone focuses on figuring out how they did it across the street, actually putting a new plan into practice gets put on the back burner. Benchmarking can become a distraction to successful planning for your BreakOUT.

Benchmarking Benefits

Despite everything, benchmarking does offer something of real value. Benchmarking lets us hear stories... stories about how other people were able to BreakOUT of their prisons. When we hear stories about:

where they were,
where they are now,
and *how they got from one place to the other…*

… We are inspired and start to believe, "If they can do it, so can we?" Benchmarking can get us fired up and raise positive expectations about how our BreakOUT plans can be successful.

So, if you want to benchmark… fine. Get some good ideas, listen to their stories, get motivated, and then get "mapping."

Mapping From Point "A" to Point "B"

We've waited long enough. It's time to pull a plan together. As you can imagine, BreakOUT attempts without a good plan rarely lead to permanent escape. You might get away for a little while but it probably won't be long before you are dragged right back to your old prison.

Now, we aren't going to give you a step-by-step instructional guide to mapping. As leaders, mapping probably is already a tool in your arsenal. If you would like more detailed instruction on mapping, there are many, great resources (books, articles, consultants, etc.) that can help you. Our goal is to approach mapping as a tool for BreakOUT… offering you some guidance as to possible pitfalls and emphasizing mapping's great value in helping you and those you work with get out of jail.

Before mapping, you basically have to know three things.

1.   Know where you are
2.   Know where you want to go
3.   Know what it will take to get you there

> **Map /'m a p/**
>
> **1 a :** a representation usually of a flat surface of the whole or part of an area **b :** conventionalized representation of spatial phenomena on a plane surface **c :** a visual representation of an area depicting various quantitative and qualitative facts, including boundaries, physical features, patterns, and distribution

Let's say that you are locked up in a cell on Alcatraz Island in California (as a tourist, of course) and want to escape to Disney World in Florida. Naturally, you want to map out your trip. You get your hands on a road map of the United States and first determine Point "A" in San Francisco and Point "B" in Orlando. You then step back and take a good look.

You can clearly see where you currently are and where it is you want to be. You can also see that there are an almost infinite number of ways you could get from Point "A" to Point "B." How do you choose the best route for you? You have to know your travel conditions.

Consider the following…

- What kind of transportation do you have access to? Are you going by sports car, bicycle or bus?
- How many drivers are you going to have and how many passengers?
- Is your goal to take the fastest way possible or do you want to take the more scenic route?
- Are there only a certain number of hours you can drive a day? How much time are you willing to take to make the whole trip?
- Do you need to make any stops along the way (to visit family, to rest up or just to use the bathroom)?
- What are your resources for the trip? Can you afford meals, hotel stays, loss of sleep, time away from work, etc.?
- What about your relationship(s) with driving companion(s)? Will they survive the trip (the relationships, not the people)?

Each one of these questions strongly affects how you will plan your journey from Point "A" to Point "B."

This list isn't exhaustive. There could be many other conditions for you to consider as you pick the best route for your journey. However, just as with anything else, while it is important to know your travel conditions, you can't let all of them affect your trip.

For instance, you could go so far as to plan the following:

Day 1

Driver A will drive 2.1 hours on Interstate 55 at an average speed of 60 mph for exactly 112.3 miles and will stop at the gas station off exit #12 to fill the tank with 12 gallons of regular unleaded gasoline at $1.90 a gallon.

Driver B will then drive the next 3.6 miles at an average speed of 35 mph to Smithsville where all three drivers will have a 22-minute lunch at the Road Kill Café. Driver A will have a hamburger, Driver B will have the stew and Driver C will have coffee only. The cost per person for lunch will be $16.78 plus a 12 percent tip.

Driver C will then drive... (Continue *ad naseum*)

Mapping a trip like this would take longer than the trip itself. Planning should take into account the specific conditions you are traveling under but not be so structured that it limits your options. You can be specific but there is a point of diminishing returns.

Good mapping takes an ability to prioritize the things that are most important to getting you from where you are to where you want to be.

B<small>REAK</small>OUT

High-Octane 80/20 Fuel

In 1897, Italian economist Vilfredo Pareto found a bizarre consistency between the distribution of wealth and income in societies. No matter which country he looked at or time period he studied, Pareto found that there was always a small minority of individuals at the top who held the majority of the wealth. The ratio of wealth to people almost always balanced out with 80 percent of wealth being owned by only 20 percent of people.

In the years that followed, others took the Pareto 80/20 Principle and eventually broadened its scope to a point where it became an empirical law that 80 percent of all results flow from only 20 percent of causes. In his book, **The 80/20 Individual**, Richard Koch writes:

> *There is no magic in the 80 and 20.... The point is that the world in not 50/50; effort and reward are not linearly related.*

> *Most of the universe consists of meaningless noise, which can drown out those few forces that are tremendously powerful and productive.*

Mapping falls under the power of the 80/20 principle, as well. Out of all of the things that could get you from Point "A" to Point "B," 20 percent of them will determine the success of your trip. The problem is identifying that 20 percent. That's the hard part. And that's the part you, as the leader, have to figure out.

The High Payoff "20%" Question Game

To help you do this, imagine for a moment that you could hire the four best thinkers in the world to help you for a week. Assume that they know more than anyone else about the industry or discipline you are trying to focus on. Two are intimately familiar with your organization and industry and the other two bring a more objective, outside perspective to the table. All four are internationally recognized. What specific questions or goals would you have these four brainiacs work on during that week? How would you utilize this incredible opportunity?

Many of us get stuck on this question because the first things that come to mind usually wouldn't be worth even bringing up to our little think tank group. Yet, aren't those same things where you spend a lot of your brain time on? The brain trust question reminds us that there is a bigger picture out there. It reminds us to be careful not to be so incremental in our thinking that we make very limited use of the talent available.

The secret to finding the 20 percent of causes that will get you where you want to go is thinking big thoughts… creative thoughts… BreakOUT thoughts. That will get you there faster than anything else.

B<small>REAK</small>OUT

Asking For Directions

If you have ever gone online and used a web mapping tool to get directions to some place you have never been before, you know it can be very helpful. But, have you ever tried using that same mapping tool to get directions to some place you already know how to get to? Most of the time, the directions you get aren't the way that you would have come up with yourself.

You see, when you are more familiar with the territory, you know where traffic tends to jam up, where there is construction that might slow you down, where there is a good shortcut, etc. It's basic common sense. If you want to get somewhere quickly and easily, check with a local who knows the area.

Now realize that as a leader, you are somewhat of an out-of-towner when it comes to certain areas in your territory. You may not always know the best way to go yourself. As you map your BreakOUT, you will want to check with the locals about the best way to get to where you are going through their "towns" (be they a region, division, department or area of expertise). Make sure you get their input while you map.

And these locals don't necessarily have to be within your organization. Sometimes the locals are the outside experts who have a lot of knowledge about a new territory you are moving into. Their objective guidance and advice can also be very valuable to you as you plot your way because they can see things more clearly (i.e., they aren't held back by the same PCC's you are).

To get the very best advice from your locals (be they internal or external resources) you must convince them you are committed to a real BreakOUT. In other words, this is not simply another "initiative." Initiative fatigue may well be the greatest road block to real BreakOUT in organizations today.

In many organizations the people at the lower levels have been exposed to so many "latest and greatest" initiatives, they are literally numb. People simply comply and go along with new initiatives with neither their heads nor their hearts fully engaged in the game. Or, they just stay low and say, "This, too, shall pass."

Not Just Where... Who?

This book is about unleashing the power of human capital (i.e. people)... not maps. Mapping is more than knowing what roads to take. It's about knowing who will help you along the way. If a map is a "network" of roads than it is also a network of people... people who will help you get where you need to go.

In a prison BreakOUT, rarely does an escapee get out without help from others. There are usually a number of co-conspirators who provide vital assistance on the journey. Some may be on the outside helping us make our escape. Most will be on the inside.

But, you have an added problem. You aren't just trying to BreakOUT on your own... you need those you lead to follow you out. When it comes to leadership, the trick is not deciding that you want to BreakOUT – it's convincing those around you to come along. Remember the story of Papillion from Chapter 1? In the end, Papillion couldn't get his friend Louis to BreakOUT with him. He had to go it alone.

For most of us, going it alone is not an option. When we are leading a group of people, we need everyone on board and moving forward. Stragglers could hold all of us back. So, once you have your BreakOUT map, the question becomes how do you get people to want to make the trip?

Getting Everyone To Enjoy The Ride

The fact is, some people will be reluctant to take the trip from Point "A" to Point "B"(reakOUT). BreakOUT isn't easy and remember that our prisons can be quite hard to see and very comfortable – allowing us to feel safe in a rapidly changing and dangerous world. Many of those that need to make the ride with you may not see the potential rewards that can be reaped by risking BreakOUT.

Basically, BreakOUT is about embracing change. In order to escape our prisons, we have to change how we think and how we act. And for many of us, the prospect of change is not a comfortable idea... especially when it seems to be forced upon us by someone else.

As the leader of your group's escape, you will face some difficult challenges in terms of getting everyone on board with your BreakOUT plan. There are two main reasons why people will resist a leader's plan to BreakOUT.

1. "Why move? I'm comfortable here, thank you."
2. "Do you have any idea how much I've invested in the status quo?"

"Why Move? I'm Comfortable Here, Thank You!"

Remember back to Chapter 5 when we told the tale of Andy Mochan and how he chose to jump from a burning oil platform into a dangerous, cold sea in order to survive. If Andy hadn't seen the fire burning all around him, he would never have jumped. If he hadn't seen that his PCC (Premature Cognitive Commitment) of "I would never jump 15 stories from an oil platform" wasn't always true, he would not be alive today.

For Andy, the burning platform was a dramatic wake up call that maintaining the status quo (staying on the burning platform) was no longer an option. Leadership during a BreakOUT is convincing people that the status quo is no longer an option and further convincing them they can capitalize on the change.

Remember the saying, "Feel the heat or see the light?" That is what a leader must do – get his or her people to both "feel the heat" and "see the light." To help motivate people to change, first you have to make them see change as necessary for their continued success and/or survival. They must be convinced that the status quo is no longer an option and that BreakOUT change is the only way to go.

But, it is also a leader's responsibility to show how change will make things better than they are now... not worse. By helping people "see the light," a leader can ease the tension of transition, allowing people to look forward to their new existence.

In his book, **Changing Minds: The Art and Science of Changing Our Own and Other People's Minds,** Howard Gardner encourages us to *"search for the resonance"* and *"stamp out the resistance."* In what he calls "early representation," Gardner presents an existing PCC like "bigger is better." He then offers an alternative "better representation," that "Smaller can be beautiful... The behemoths of one era may well become the dinosaurs of the next." In effect, Gardner suggests that when we attempt to change the minds both of ourselves and others, we work to identify what "resonates" with us and move past what makes us "resist" in terms of new ideas and ways of doing things.

Finally, leaders can also help ease the transition by keeping some familiar things around even after the change is complete.

For instance, when the light bulb was first introduced, manufacturers still put the old lampshades on the new light bulbs so as to keep a sense of comfort and continuity during the transition from candle-power to kilowatt-hour.

Some leaders will face more difficult challenges than others in helping their people to BreakOUT. Successful organizations might not have as far to go to get from where they are to where they want to be, but it's hard to feel the heat to change when things are already going pretty well. On the other hand, major BreakOUTs can be achieved by organizations and industries who are in big trouble because they feel the "heat." We might like to think we are motivated by "seeing the light," but the harsh reality is that most major BreakOUTs are a result of "feeling the heat."

"Do You Have Any Idea How Much I've Invested In The Status Quo?"

This argument against change is all about people's investment in the old system. People like to build on what they have done before. We have all put a great deal of effort and energy into getting where we are now. The idea of leaving much or all of this behind as we move forward is very discomforting.

If you have ever watched a television show called, ***Clean Sweep***, on The Learning Channel, it is an amazing example of how we get attached to the things we invested in over time. On ***Clean Sweep***, homeowners invite the TV team in to help them reorganize certain rooms in their homes and help them clear out things that might no longer be needed.

Each show, you see how an amazing pile of what looks like junk is taken out of the various rooms and dumped on a large tarp in the back yard. The homeowners are then challenged to quickly sort through their stuff and place everything in either the "Keep" area, the "Sell" area, or the "Trash" area.

Almost inevitably, at the end of the allotted time, the homeowners have a couple of pieces in the "Sell" area, practically nothing in the "Trash" area and have moved most of their original pile into the "Keep" area.

Despite the fact that they invited a crew of people to come in to help them clear things out, their initial resistance to parting with their things is incredibly strong – mostly because they have, in the past, invested either time, money or sentiment into all their stuff. It takes an "organization expert," to challenge them, push them and even force the homeowners to give up their old "junk" to move the process along. However, at the end of the show, almost every homeowner is completely relieved and even freed by letting go of their old stuff and having their homes reorganized in a totally new way. It is a very interesting exercise moving others toward BreakOUT.

Leaders have to establish a sense of ownership and reward to get people to buy into the BreakOUT plan. Rather than leaving their old investment behind, people have to see that they will get bigger and better rewards when they emerge on the other side of change. And don't forget, if you show the promise of a better tomorrow as a result of your BreakOUT plan, make sure that when you get where you want to be, you fulfill your promise and take time to celebrate your successful escape.

Big BreakOUTs Versus Baby BreakOUTs

As a final word on mapping in terms of working toward BreakOUT, we want to encourage you once again to think big. BreakOUT is risky. It takes courage and an open mind. In the process of mapping BreakOUT, is very easy to get stuck in the trap of incremental change... taking baby steps toward our goals instead of reaching for the stars.

For example, a person could say, "I want to quit smoking," and map out a BreakOUT plan that would get them from where they are now (smoking two packs a day) to where they want to be (not smoking at all). This is a great goal. It is very challenging and requires a great deal of effort, discipline and focus and the resulting reward would be very beneficial. But is it a "big" BreakOUT?

What if, instead of saying "I want to quit smoking," a person said, "I will live a healthful, positive life of purpose!" How does this change the degree of BreakOUT?

Don't limit yourself to how far you can go to escape your prison. You can move toward change incrementally (step-by-step) or you can change transformationally (taking your life, your organization and your team to a whole new level). Transformational BreakOUT is really what will unleash the power of people… setting them free from prison to soar to new and untold heights.

> "Come to the edge."
> "We can't. We are afraid."
>
> "Come to the edge."
> "We can't. We will fall!"
>
> "Come to the edge."
>
> And they came.
> And he pushed them.
>
> And they flew.
>
> – Guillaume Apollinaire

Mapping: The Five Things

Done well, mapping accomplishes five things:

1. It starts with a big, bold vision of the destination. In the beginning it may be the vision of one but eventually everyone needs to share the vision.

2. It focuses on the customers and how the customers see the organization.

3. It is done in a way that allows and encourages all employees from executive to line personnel to have buy-in to the finished product.

4. It helps all employees to understand how their individual work adds value and instills pride in their total performance.

5. It is a holistic approach that explores in detail the inter-relationships of processes.

B<small>REAK</small>OUT

Part III:

B<small>REAK</small>OUT

Creating A Workplace of Choice: BreakOUT Human Capital Practices

BreakOUT

Chapter 8
Workplaces of Choice
(BreakOUT Practices That Work)

Showing people that you value them one-on-one takes skill, practice and heart. Showing people that you value them as a group or team can be even trickier. So, how can you do it? How do you, as a leader, compound the human capital on your team?

Well, we decided to take a look at those companies who have earned a spot on Fortune's annual list of the "100 Best Companies To Work For." These are companies who are ranked high by their own employees. Over 46,000 randomly selected employees from 304 candidate companies complete an employee-opinion survey which, along with a company questionnaire, is combined to give a company a total "best place to work" score.

Sounds good, doesn't it? These places should be great breeding grounds for motivated, energized, and engaged workers – ones who would be open to BreakOUT and driven to reach new levels of productivity, creativity and success. That's what we thought. These companies even have a new name – Workplaces of Choice.

As we began to look at the organizations that make the top of the ***Choice*** list, we noticed one thing immediately. Organizational culture plays a big role in distinguishing a "great place to work."

There is a signature correlation between happy and engaged employees and a great organizational culture. Makes sense, doesn't it? Culture would definitely impact whether employees thrive or dive. They each have their unique traditions, beliefs, structures and ways of doing things.

Culture /'k&l-ch&r/

1 a : the set of shared attitudes, values, goals, and practices that characterizes a company or corporation   **b :** the integrated pattern of human knowledge, belief, and behavior that depends upon an individual's capacity for learning and transmitting knowledge to succeeding generations

---

Using this list of ***Choice*** companies, we decided to look at what the leaders in these companies did to help create a "Workplace of Choice." We've done the research, sorted through the policies, programs, philosophies and plans and have come up with a series of leadership practices that seem to most directly affect the building and sustaining of a strong Human Capital focused culture of ***Choice***.

We have divided these BreakOUT Human Capital Practices into four categories:

- BreakOUT Envisioning Practices
- BreakOUT Alignment Practices
- BreakOUT Engagement Practices
- BreakOUT Culture Practices

We should note that many of these practices are not new. There may be a few that you haven't seen before but most have been talked and written about for years. The difference is in how organizations implement these practices. When it comes to a Workplace of Choice, telling people that they have great value to the organization is much more than just lip service. Human capital truly has value... and it keeps its value even when times are tough. So many organizations talk a good game when it comes to valuing their employees, but when push comes to shove and times get tough, employees know that they are going to end up with the short end of the stick.

As you read over the following BreakOUT Human Capital Practices, consider those practices new to you as tools you could add to your repertoire to help you inspire your people to do their jobs better. As for those practices you are already familiar with and maybe already think you are using well, take a really good look at exactly how you are implementing these practices. Are you really using them to strengthen the human capital on your team... or are they just hanging out there in a weak attempt to appear people-focused?

Think of the BreakOUT Human Capital Practices like muscles. They don't help you much if they are weak from lack of use.

Muscles need to be put to work in order to increase strength and durability. That is the key to real BreakOUT.

In the following chapters, we will go through each practice, one by one, showing you how to use these strategies to create a culture for your team that is *Choice*.

BreakOUT Human Capital Practices	
Envisioning Practices	**Alignment Practices**
1. Vision	5. Gaining Commitment
2. Stretch Goals	6. Transparent Score Keeping
3. Mapping	7. Stretch Assignments
4. Storytelling	8. High Value Training & Education
Engagement Practices	**Culture Practices**
9. Financial Incentives	15. Status Neutral Culture
10. Selective & Secure Employment	16. Learning & Innovation Culture
11. Peer Interviewing	17. Flexible Flextime Culture
12. Decentralized Decision-Making	18. No Secrets Culture
13. Spontaneous Task-Focused Teams	19. No Excuses Culture
14. Leader Rounding	20. Celebration Culture

Chapter 9
BreakOUT Envisioning Practices
(The Blind Leading The Blind No More)

Before anyone can BreakOUT of anything, they have to see where it is they are... and see where it is they want to be. When it comes to leading groups of people, there is sometimes the unfortunate event of the blind leading the blind. Leaders without truly clear direction are leading people who also don't know where it is they are trying to go... but everyone keeps working really hard to get there.

As we detailed in Chapter 3, self-awareness about who you are and where you are – be it for an individual or an organization – is vital to breaking out of your PCC prison. But equally important is knowing where you want to be and having an executable plan to get there. This is where many people (and organizations) fall short.

One of the reasons many of us get "stuck" in our lives is because a) we can't really see where it is we want to be... or b) if we do, we don't quite know how to get there **in our own way**.

When it comes to "a)," we get stuck in the status quo because, despite all of its faults, we are used to it and have become a bit too comfortable. We don't even want to think about getting out because we have our heads under the blankets and are choosing to ignore the alarm blaring just out of reach telling us it's time to wake up and make a change.

As for "b)," even if we did dream of a place where we want to be, we sometimes just don't know how to get from here to there… and doing it **in our own way**. From losing ten pounds to building a multinational company, we can all research dozens of different ways that other people have used to get from A to B. The problem is, others aren't you. You have to come up with a way that will work best for you and, again, so often we get "stuck" right here with no plan to get there.

So, the following Envisioning strategies are designed not to tell you "what" you should do, but to have you tell yourself what it is you want to do and how to get there. More than that, the term "envision" actually means "to picture oneself." These envisioning strategies don't just show you where you want to be and how to get there; they let you picture yourself already there. You see yourself enjoying the fruits of your BreakOUT which, is one of the best motivators to get out from under the covers there is.

So, let's take a look at our four BreakOUT Human Capital Practices that are Envisioning Practices.

1. Vision
2. Stretch Goals
3. Mapping
4. Storytelling

Envisioning Practices

BreakOUT H.C. Practice 1 – Vision

Create a vision that inspires, motivates, and guides your people.

Many business leaders "talk" endlessly about vision, and your organization probably has its own version of a vision or a mission statement. But does it address and engage your employees? Is it simply a plaque that hangs on the wall or is it a living statement that is felt in the hearts and minds of every employee – a statement that connects them and inspires them to rally to a common cause? Usually, if employees are mentioned at all, they're not addressed as important players. This fact is astonishing considering that if any company (or any group of people) ever hopes to achieve the goals it has for the future, it'll be their employees who will get them there. Not customers. Not shareholders. Employees. All of them.

Look at it in terms of the Equity Equation. People give to get (see Chapter 4). If people are going to jump out of bed ready to hit the ground running each morning, to give their best, they need to know where it is that they're running to. They need a point of destination – an oasis on the horizon. Without it, people feel they are working very hard and getting nowhere.

A vision is a powerful motivator for any organization or team when all employees feel a part of it. They have to understand that what they're doing by "living the vision" directly impacts your organization's success.

By making the vision come alive for every member of your organization, you'll be on your way to creating a Workplace of Choice.

BreakOUT Vision Questions

❑ Have I communicated the vision in a way that is meaningful to all employees?

❑ What am I going to do to engender a feeling of ownership in the vision for all employees?

❑ What actions have I taken to create a shared vision among all employees?

❑ Is there a gap between the organization's vision and how it acts every day?

❑ How do we make sure that the vision is more than a plaque on the wall?

Envisioning Practices

BreakOUT H.C. Practice 2 – Stretch Goals

Set goals for yourself and your team that stretch further and higher than you even think possible.

Do you think big? Do you dream the impossible dream? Probably not. You might think you do… but, trust us, you don't. Only very few people do. If you want to run a comparison test, measure you own BreakOUT goals to that of our friend Henri "Papillion" Charriere. Does your goal compel you to jump off a cliff into dangerous, shark-infested waters with your only support being a bag of coconuts and a dream of freedom?

Now, there is nothing wrong with setting small(er) goals. Just know you'll be getting small(er) results. But that is not what this book is about. This book is about BreakOUT, which means stretching beyond our current ideas about goal setting and setting the mark higher than we think we might be able to go… in fact, that's the exact idea.

In 1994, Jim Collins and Jerry Porra's published their classic business book, **Built To Last**. In it, they introduced the concept of BHAGs – Big, Hairy, Audacious Goals (pronounced bee-hags). This witty acronym emphasized the need for organizations (and individuals) to really break the mold in terms of how they set goals for themselves.

Notice, Collins and Porra's didn't suggest making RWPGs – Realistic, Well-groomed, Proportional Goals (pronounced with difficulty), which is how most of us approach goal setting. We tend to choose making a "comfortable living" over being "obnoxiously wealthy." We will opt to "write a book" instead of "write an international best seller." We set goals in keeping with what we "think" can happen versus what might be possible.

Why do we do this?

Can you guess why?
Yep! Those pesky PCC's like to limit us here again.

Premature cognitive commitments love to kick into high gear when it comes to deciding what it is we want to achieve now and into the future. PCC's tell us that only certain things are doable, possible, realistic, etc. Yet, life as we know it today exists because people achieved the impossible – harnessing electricity, the advent of vaccines, crossing the ocean, etc. It is actually in our nature to explore, stretch beyond our known limits and reach for the stars. Most of us just don't tap the depth of that potential.

We like the term BHAG because the terminology itself helps blow the doors off our PCC prison and forces us to stretch our neck out in terms of what we want and what we could achieve.

As a leader, it is part of your job to set the stretch goals for your team. Leaders have to be the ones who climb up out of the desert to the top of the mountain, see past all the obstacles and challenges (and PCC's) to point to the ocean far off in the distance and say, "Let's go for a swim."

When working to come up with stretch goals, let the sky be the limit. If first you think, "We are going to get a 100 of something," stop yourself and add a zero… or a bunch of them. If you find yourself balking at setting your sights higher, ask yourself why. You'll probably unearth a few PCC's there.

Then push them aside and really go for those big, hairy, audacious goals.

It's like Nike saying back in the 1960's that they wanted to be the largest sports and fitness company in the world. Twenty years later, they were just that. It's like Citicorp saying they want to service one billion customers worldwide. It might take them another 10 years but they are well on their way. And, it's like the biggest BHAG in recent time – standing up in front of the world and saying that the United States of America is going to put a man on the moon and making it happen in just eight years!

BreakOUT Stretch Goal Questions

❑ What are your goals for yourself and your team?

❑ How could you stretch your goals further (i.e., do they meet the BHAG test)?

❑ Are there any PCC's stopping you from setting your sights higher – either for yourself or your organization?

Envisioning Practices
BreakOUT H.C. Practice 3 – Mapping
Devise a plan to get from A to B(reakOUT).

BreakOUT

Having a feeling of déjà vu? If you've read Chapter 9, this is quite understandable. Already well versed in mapping, you can easily understand (and put into practice) this highly valuable envisioning strategy.

If you haven't read Chapter 9 and are interested in mapping as an Envisioning strategy, we recommend you make a U-turn to head back and check it out.

Envisioning Practices
BreakOUT H.C. Practice 4 – Storytelling
Use storytelling as a delivery system for communicating vision and motivating action toward reaching desired goals.

A disgruntled woman stomped into a department store fuming from both ears, very upset that the tires she purchased did not meet her expectations. As she aggressively walked up to the sales counter, with both hands on her hips, she demanded her money back from the clerk. Although she did not have a sales receipt, the woman recalled exactly what she paid for the tires. The clerk politely gave her a full refund and apologized for the inconvenience as all coworkers looked on in amazement. The woman left as a satisfied customer not knowing that the store did not sell tires.

How many times do you think that story has been told and retold as the ultimate example of customer service within that organization? Stories stick… and they spread. Can't you just see the unhappy customer in our story? How clearly is the message of service excellence communicated? Do you think you will ever forget it? Will you maybe tell it to someone else? Storytelling is thought to be one of our most powerful forms of human communication and has been used for thousands of years. Those who use it effectively, loudly profess its power. Storytelling can be used to teach, motivate, and entertain. When used correctly, it can be an extraordinary way to make certain that your vision is understood, shared and communicated to everyone on your team.

People remember them (especially the good ones) and tell them over and over again. Most of human knowledge was kept in the manner of stories for thousands of years and, despite all of our advances in the recording and transferring of information, most people are still far more inclined to listen to someone tell a good story than analyze a digitally rendered pie chart.

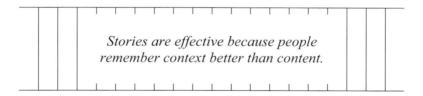

> *Stories are effective because people*
> *remember context better than content.*

If you want to use storytelling to your advantage, take a walk around your organization and listen – *really listen* – to the conversations your people have. What are the stories they tell? Do these stories share the appropriate values and vision for your team? How might you make them better? What about your customers' stories? What do they say about you?

If storytelling does not come naturally to you, don't worry. There is a skill to storytelling and it can be learned. There are many books that can teach you how. Or, the next time you need to communicate an important message to someone, take a moment to see if you could couch it in terms of a story.

If you are not yet "sold" on the value of storytelling, conduct your own informal research project. Share information in your regular way. Next, weave the information into a story that you can share. Tell your story. Return to your subjects a few days later and determine who recalls the information more accurately. *Choice* organizations have their own stories and they are told often everywhere. What are yours?

BreakOUT Storytelling Questions

- ❑ Do you have a story that communicates the vision of the organization?

- ❑ Do your stories impact peoples thinking and their emotions?

- ❑ What are the stories that you hear repeated across the organization? Are they positive or negative?

Chapter 10
BreakOUT Alignment Practices
(NOT Every Which Way You Can)

A strong vision is the first step in engaging people to perform their best. The second step is making sure that the work being done day-to-day, all of the policies, procedures, and processes in your company, are aligned with that vision. For employees, there is nothing worse than coming into work and knowing that the meeting they have to go to that day or the reports that they have to fill out at the end of each quarter, do nothing to actually achieve any real business goals. You have to "connect-the-dots" in a meaningful way so employees understand how their contributions affect business.

Even worse is when company policies become barriers – requiring many time consuming and cumbersome practices that they actually prevent employees from doing what they really need to do in order to achieve organizational goals.

The following practices can be used by leaders to help build stronger alignment between their overall vision and the actual work executed day-to-day on-the-job.

So, let's take a look at our four BreakOUT Human Capital Practices that are Alignment Practices.

5. Gaining Commitment
6. Transparent Score Keeping
7. Stretch Assignments
8. High Value Training & Education

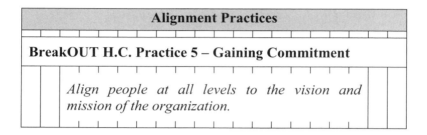

Alignment Practices
BreakOUT H.C. Practice 5 – Gaining Commitment
Align people at all levels to the vision and mission of the organization.

Committed people have both their heads and their hearts in the game. They are stakeholders. Their chips are on the table and they play to win. But how does a leader inspire people to commit to a vision? You don't just snap your fingers and say, "Let's do it!"

At one of the Workplaces of Choice we know well, we discovered a fascinating practice. They're a hospital and every time a patient comes into the hospital, they are given a "Welcome" letter from the president of the Hospital. Sounds simple so far, doesn't it?

Well, at the bottom of the letter, there is a closing line that reads, "If you want to discuss your care, please let a staff member know your thoughts, or call me at 555-2323 (office) or 555-4545 (home)."

Think about this for a minute.

The president of the hospital gives every patient coming into the hospital his direct office number **and** his home telephone number. How many leaders do you know who would give all of their customers their home phone number? Talk about taking the "Can I speak to your supervisor" tactic to a whole new level.

The beauty of the approach used by the president of the hospital is that it is a strong, clear example to everyone (leadership, employees and customers) that the organization is totally committed to their goal of unparalleled customer service. That is his vision and he stands behind it.

Not only is the president putting himself and his personal time on the line, imagine how hospital employees react to this letter. If it were you and you knew that you customers had direct access to the head of your organization, how would it affect your behavior on the job? Hopefully, not at all but you get the point. Your commitment level would certainly get a boost and wouldn't you also be conducting business in line with the organization's vision and goals?

Even if the letter idea isn't a workable one with your team, it is an interesting practice to give some thought to what you would want to have in place before you gave your clients direct access to you – 24 hours a day, seven days a week.

B<small>REAK</small>OUT

	BreakOUT Gaining Commitment Questions	

- ❑ What are you doing to engage the hearts and minds of your employees?

- ❑ What reasons does the organization give to employees to be committed beyond the paycheck?

- ❑ How committed do you think your people are in your organization?

- ❑ What could you do to build commitment into your organization?

- ❑ What would you want to have in place at work before you gave your home telephone number out to each and every one of your customers?

Alignment Practices

BreakOUT H.C. Practice 6 –Transparent Score Keeping

Have widespread sharing of financial and performance information in formats that lets everyone know the score.

Why do most of us love to watch and play various sports and games? We like to win. How do we know we are winning? We keep score.

Imagine you're playing a game where you had no way of knowing if you are winning or losing the game – playing tennis without a net, playing football without goal posts or yard line markers, etc. If you never knew whether you were winning or losing, how motivated would you be to take risks, go after a big play or devise a winning strategy? If you never knew the score, how long would you keep playing before you got bored, frustrated and walked away? Not long.

While most of us realize the importance of keeping score when it comes to sports and games, it's amazing how many leaders try and win without ever telling their players the score. Many employees show up to work each day without knowing whether their team is winning or losing. Developing a clear and easily understood score keeping system – and setting measurable goals – is the key to keeping peoples' "heads in the game." Unless they are so far behind that they are out of the game, people tend to play harder when they know the score and what they have to do to win.

So, what exactly is "transparent score keeping?" It's measuring the critical behaviors that can help or hurt the bottom-line in ways that are:

- Simple
- Clear
- And easy for all to see

Basically, a transparent score keeping system is like a scoreboard at a football game – an easy way to see the most essential information about the game. In a flash, you'll know the current score, the time remaining to play, and how many time outs the team has left. You only need to take a quick look at the board to know who is winning the game and who isn't.

Everyone on your team needs to be motivated to win the game and to keep doing things that will help them win the game. Again, go back to the Equity Equation. If employees give their hard work, their skills, and their commitment, they deserve to get feedback on their performance in a timely and easily understood format. That's what transparent score keeping is all about.

BreakOUT Transparent Score Keeping Questions

- Is everyone on your team aware of your critical success factors and how they are measured?

- Are the scores (measurements) consistently communicated?

- What happens when you see a negative trend or dip in the scores?

- Do you know the score?

- If you walked out your office door right now and asked four of the people on your team the score... could they answer? Would they even know what you are talking about?

- Do your people know how their efforts affect the score?

Alignment Practices

BreakOUT H.C. Practice 7 –Stretch Assignments

Employee development through carefully selected on-the-job "stretch & growth" assignments supported by mentoring and coaching.

Over the years, we have asked hundreds of successful leaders in all types of companies one very basic question: "As you look back, what has contributed most to your growth and development as a leader?" Far and away the most frequent answer is "…when I was given a stretch assignment."

Stretch assignments are challenging jobs that are given to employees so that they may "stretch" their skills and abilities to levels not achieved before. Stretch assignments present new and difficult challenges to people. They're tough. But, if employees survive and complete these assignments successfully, they are rewarded with greater confidence in their leadership ability as well as having learned new skills.

In study after study, people say that they learn most effectively while they are on-the-job. If challenging tasks push the limits of the employee's knowledge and abilities, then the company as well as the employee benefit enormously.

Many companies already utilize stretch assignments quite effectively. A recent study by McKinsey & Company entitled *Winning the War for Talent*, asked managers how effective their particular company was at utilizing stretch assignments as a development tool. Most executives gave their companies a very high rating.

However, not all stretch assignments end well, especially if handled badly. They are often stress-filled and can lead a once high potential employee to ruin. Leaders cannot simply throw their people into tough positions and then simply expect them to do well. They need to offer support to their employees and help them either learn or develop the skills necessary to do the job right. What's the key? Most leaders say that the difference between success and failure during a stretch assignment is the availability of coaching and feedback from their immediate leader.

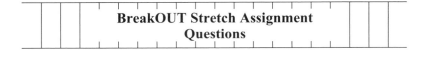

BreakOUT Stretch Assignment Questions

❑ Do I look beyond current capabilities of employees to their potential, then help build that potential?

❑ What kind of assignments could I offer that would "stretch" members of my team?

❑ How would I support/coach/mentor team members while they were working through a "stretch" assignment?

Alignment Practices
BreakOUT H.C. Practice 8 – High Value Training & Education
Provide training and education programs aligned with business goals that maximize overall performance, enhance employee marketability, and promote long-term employee relationships and loyalty.

If a company closely aligns training and education programs with business goals, they can make certain their employees are kept up to speed on the skills and knowledge necessary for the company to be successful and prosperous. That's one benefit. But, high value training and educational programs can also be an equitable compromise companies can offer their employees. While it is now nearly impossible for companies to promise their people "employment for life," they can promise employees they will keep them employable – providing appropriate training and education that will allow employees to broaden and improve their own skills. This training and education enhances people's performance in their current job, but also keeps them competitive in the marketplace. So, if employee and company do part paths, the company has at least equipped that person to land another good job.

There's also a bonus for those companies genuinely trying to build long-term relationships with their employees. Data from the 1999 Emerging Workforce Study shows that 41 percent of employees who say their company offers poor training plan to look for another job within 12 months. But just 12 percent of those who rated training opportunities as excellent within their organizations expected to jump ship. As many companies know, high turnover isn't cheap. That same survey pegged the cost of losing the typical worker at $50,000.

When times are good, most companies do a reasonable job of providing quality training and educational programs to their employees. However, when the economy gets iffy, training and education programs are among the first casualties on the cost-cutting chopping block.

Before you cut training and education, consider if the money you save will outweigh the equity cost to your employees. Is it better to prove to your employees that you value them enough to continue growing their knowledge and skill levels or do you want to risk alienating them and losing their top performance?

BreakOUT High Value Training & Education Questions

❑ How are you investing in the growth and development of your employees?

❑ Are you providing the education and training necessary for employees to excel in a changing environment?

❑ Is training and development valued by the organization? How is this visible to employees?

❑ Is this training beneficial to my team both now and into their professional future?

❑ How highly do I value training and education as part of the culture I am building with my team?

Chapter 11
BreakOUT Engagement Practices
(How To Get People To Say "I Do")

You've got your vision. You've got things in line with that vision. What's next? (Note: This is key). If there is one area where most organizations struggle, it is in engaging their people to actually get the job done… manifesting vision into real success. This next series of practices – Engagement Practices – are used to motivate people to stay on top of their game, every day.

So, let's take a look at the six BreakOUT Human Capital Practices that are Engagement Practices.

9.   Financial Incentives
10.   Selective & Secure Employment
11.   Peer Interviewing
12.   Decentralized Decision Making
13.   Spontaneous Task-Focused Teams
14.   Leader Rounding

Engagement Practices

BreakOUT H.C. Practice 9 – Financial Incentives

> *Offer competitive pay with financial incentives that are driven deep into the organization – everyone gets to share. Reward not only good execution, but innovation, as well.*

Pay is still the primary reason most of us get out of bed in the morning to face the hours of work ahead of us. No one would want to deny the power money has to prompt and reward terrific performance. Indeed, many corporations already offer financial incentives, but usually only to the top people in the organization – primarily, CEOs and other top-level executives reap the rewards that come from strong corporate performance.

According to a 2004 University of Pennsylvania study, in 2004, the average CEO of a major corporation earned more then 400 times that of the average factory worker. When people perceive an imbalance in equity – and pay certainly is the kind of imbalance that shows up very quickly on their radar screens – it drastically reduces their willingness to perform. It saps their willingness to do their jobs fully and well. If people aren't motivated to excel at their jobs, performance doesn't skyrocket, it sputters, and the bottom line suffers accordingly. But, for those companies – few though they may be – who have realized the power of distributing financial incentives across the organization, they have watched their bottom lines flourish.

The concepts of competitive pay and financial incentives have to be driven so deeply into the organization that even the people at the lowest levels have a chance to reap the benefits. All employees – from the mailroom to the executive suite – have to feel that if their team or their company does well, then they themselves will get a slice of the pie. That's what financial equity means to you, doesn't it? If that's what it means to you, then why would the people who report to you, or the people who report to them, feel any differently?

Oh, there's a little foreshadowing here. Check out BreakOUT H.C. Practice 16 – the one about cultivating an environment that values, recognizes and rewards learning and innovation. Well, don't just make those words sound pretty. Back them up with hard cash. People should get good bucks for creativity and innovation as well as for the number of transmissions produced by an assembly line or the number of computers shipped.

			BreakOUT Financial Incentives Questions			

❏ Are the financial incentives I am offering among the best compared to others in the industry?

❏ Do I offer financial incentives all the way down the line? Why or why not?

❏ What are the potential benefits of pushing financial incentives to all levels of the organization?

❏ Are the financial incentives I am offering linked to any other non-financial rewards?

Engagement Practices									
BreakOUT H.C. Practice 10 – Selective & Secure Employment									
		Promote long-term employee relationships and loyalty through selective, lean and focused hiring.							

You may have heard the adage, "hire the best and fire the worst." In reality, most companies do much better at "hiring the best" than they do at "firing the worst."

Again, it's actually a matter of equity. If your very best people see that your organization is willing to tolerate substandard work from other people around them, and these people get to stay on the job, that fact sends a message, and it is this: "Lousy work tolerated here!"

Not the most inspiring message, is it? All it does is get your very best people to take the edge off performances that used to be razor-sharp. If the organization doesn't care enough about the quality of the work to toss out the people who don't do the job, then why should the people who can do the job well make the effort?

In addition, providing some sense of employment security is absolutely vital for motivating people to perform their very best. Employees who are distracted by worries over what will happen to them if they lose their job simply can't focus on doing their best work. Lean and selective hiring requires that organizations, yours included, fill empty slots with the utmost care and consideration. It's essential to comb through roles and responsibilities inside the organization constantly, then decide which jobs are essential and who the best people are to fill them.

We advise teams and companies to retool themselves often. By trying to create new synergies between existing roles and responsibilities, an organization can beef up its effectiveness. At the same time, they can give employees a chance to stretch their talents and create an even larger number of skills and wider experience in the process.

For example, if a position opens up, don't automatically fill it. First, ask the people in the same area whether the job is really needed or if there's a more effective way to get the job done. If the work can be consolidated among existing employees or several open positions combined into just a few new ones, the people taking on the work must be compensated for the extra work. If employees are willing to help save the company money by doing more, then they should be rewarded. That's one way financial equity is distributed among your people, along with the new responsibilities. Getting more pay for helping have fewer jobs is one way to make sure that selective, lean hiring actually works.

You are trying to build the best team possible to help you manifest your vision. Take the time and make the effort to do it well.

	BreakOUT Selective & Secure Employment Questions	

❑ Do you take the time needed to fully evaluate the lead applicants or do you rush to fill a position?

❑ Do you push to meet the "time to fill" statistic or do you slow down the process to assure selection of the right applicant?

❑ Do you weigh the "fit" with the organization's values and culture as highly as the skill and experience of the applicant?

❑ Do you have the best people in the best positions to help you win the game?

❑ Do you exit those who aren't playing at the top of their game?

❑ If you consolidate positions, do you compensate those who are taking on the extra work?

Engagement Practices
BreakOUT H.C. Practice 11 – Peer Interviewing
Incorporate peer interviewing into your employee selection process to engage and empower employees and build team commitment.

Peer interviewing is a selection process that allows members of a work group to help evaluate job candidates and become involved in the hiring of future employees. After it has been determined that a candidate meets the initial employment requirements of the specific position, current employees become involved in the selection process to determine if the candidate "fits" the company culture and specific requirements of the job. Existing employees become part of the process through their selection of team members.

Think about it. Peer interviewing eliminates the chances that employees will say or feel "what was my boss thinking when they hired this person?" They are now part of the process and must take ownership of the results. They are more likely to look at the success of the new team member as their personal responsibility. They are empowered by being a part of the decision-making process and become engaged in making the results successful.

Job candidates also benefit from the process. They can ask questions regarding the specific position and obtain honest and realistic answers about the job requirements from people who are actually *performing* the job. Since they speak to several peers simultaneously, they can imagine themselves in daily interaction with the work group and determine if it is a comfortable "fit." They will also get a "feel" for the company's culture as they interact with several employees rather than one hiring manager.

Although the "inquisition" of several peers may appear a bit daunting at first, employees can be taught how to structure the interview session to facilitate the relaxation and comfort of the candidate. Consider "assigning" this role to someone in the group. Once communication is more relaxed, the chemistry of the work group can be checked to predict future successful relationships. Do employees share a sense of humor with easy communication? Are they more formal in their style? Will their styles compliment each other? As more teams are used to accomplish organizational goals, this "chemistry" will become even more critical in the future.

In addition to engaging and empowering your employees, there are other benefits to peer interviewing. First, if hiring decisions are perceived as fair and just, your company is likely to reap the benefit of an enhanced image within the organizational community through your use of a thorough selection system. As a result, a larger number of qualified candidates may be attracted to your organization enabling the organization to be highly selective in hiring decisions. This will be a nice problem to have in light of the changing workforce.

Second, peer interviewing is also likely to reduce costly turnover for the company. Candidates are in a better position to obtain a more realistic preview of the position and the dynamics of the team, including both the positive and negative aspects of the position. This may help them to more accurately assess the match between their personal needs and the company's needs to make a more informed decision. Candidates that are ultimately selected are likely to be a better "match."

One added note should you want to engage in peer interviewing… these structured interviews should be conducted with the same job-related questions consistently asked of all candidates so "apples can be compared to apples," not "oranges." Make certain that you run your interview questions through your human resource department as the Courts consider the interview a selection "test." Employment laws require that you cannot base a hiring decision on anything other than bona fide occupational requirements.

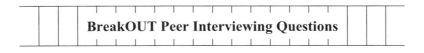

BreakOUT Peer Interviewing Questions

❑ Does your current selection process involve current employees?

❑ Do colleagues have an opportunity to provide feedback on applicants from their perspective?

❏ If feasible, how could peer interviewing benefit your hiring practice? Your organization?

Engagement Practices
BreakOUT H.C. Practice 12 – Decentralized Decision-Making
Sponsor self-managed teams with informal leadership empowered to make decisions close to the point of transaction, be it with customers, vendors or partners.

Today, change is a given. It's rampant in organizations and the marketplace. As a result, the ability to make decisions rapidly becomes absolutely vital. Wasting time frequently means wasting opportunity. Companies don't have the luxury of passing ideas up and down the corporate ladder before someone – anyone – finally makes a decision.

Instead of allowing your people to fritter away their time dithering over who will make the decision and what the decision will be, consider giving the person in your company closest to the point of transaction – whether it's with a customer, partner or vendor – the responsibility and the authority to take charge and make decisions. The people closest to the situation obviously know the most about what's going on and are best suited to make the right choices. So let them do it.

But, be warned. If you do decentralize decision-making, you must do it on a basis of trust. Don't make the same mistake many companies make. While they say they believe the people down the ladder making the decisions are, generally, making the right choices, they actually inwardly cringe at the thought of decentralizing decision-making, fearing it will lead to bad decisions. Sure there's some risk of this, but it's largely offset by the increased response time to both change and opportunity. Incidentally, just where is it carved in stone that because someone at the top makes a decision that success is guaranteed?

Trust is essential to carry off decentralization. Though many companies now mumble soothing words about how their employees are empowered, employees who exercise that power on a day-to-day basis often find themselves being overruled by their superiors in the organization. These superiors can consistently question and/or revoke the decisions their subordinates make and often, when things go bad, employees find themselves being punished for doing what they thought was their job.

With *real* trust, employees feel safe enough to attempt to find new solutions to old problems, admit mistakes, learn from those mistakes and perform beyond expectations. The concept really is simple. When employees are hired to do a job, they want to know that they're trusted to do it well. What they don't want is the uneasy feeling that just around the corner, a manager is waiting to jump on them if they actually do make decisions or something goes wrong with the decisions they've made.

BreakOUT

Employees should be held accountable for their decisions, sure. But it's only fair that the organization respect the decisions they make or provide the training/knowledge required to make the right decisions.

Again, it's a question of equity. If employees feel their intelligence and ability to make sound decisions really isn't respected or supported by their organization, they'll go back to doing just enough to get by and avoid making any decisions at all. That way they get their paychecks and take no risk. It's a safe, secure approach to keeping a job, but it also means a lot of missed opportunity for the company.

BreakOUT Decentralized Decision-Making Questions

❑ How do I encourage staff to make decisions?

❑ How do I show my support of decisions team members made?

❑ How far from the point of "contact" are decisions made on your team?

❑ Are your people empowered to make decisions?

❑ Do you support their decisions… even if they sometimes turn out to be the wrong ones?

Engagement Practices
BreakOUT H.C. Practice 13 – Spontaneous Task-Oriented Teams
Utilize spontaneous teams of diverse people to come together to develop solutions or complete tasks who then disband once their task is complete.

"Two heads are better than one." Right? Why? What is it that makes that concept of effecting "teaming" such a long-standing, high value business strategy?

The most obvious answers are that combining groups of people together leads to:

- Combined brainpower and increased intellectual stimulation
- Better use of diverse talents, knowledge and experience
- Greater involvement and commitment by all team members
- Improved decision-making

Taking a moment to note that we are talking specifically about "effective" teams here (as opposed to any dysfunctional, ineffective teams out there), most of us benefit when we have the ability to bounce ideas off of others and/or have the help of others to complete tasks. If effectively managed, teams can get things done better, faster and more easily than any one person alone.

B**reakOUT**

Let's try a little game. Fill in the blanks on the following three common statements. Do this on your own right now and only give yourself a couple of minutes to come up with answers.

- 24 H_____ in a D_____.
- 18 H_____ on a G_____ C_____.
- 200 D_____ for P_____ G_____ in M_____.

Did you get them all? Now ask someone else (a friend, spouse, co-worker or guy in the elevator) to help you. Could they "see" the ones you couldn't?

In addition to the more obvious reasons why teams can be an effective business strategy, let's think BreakOUT. Why would working in teams be a breakthrough for BreakOUT? Once again, it comes back to our PCC's. We all have our own individual premature cognitive commitments. But, whatever boundaries, blocks or limitations you might have, they are probably not the same as the other people on your team, which means that they might think of things that you can't from within your PCC prison. And, vice versa. You'll see things that they might not because of their PCC's. Teams are an excellent way to cancel out individual PCC blockages to BreakOUT into new territory.

In fact, an attempt to develop an interesting teaming format resulted in a huge BreakOUT recently. Ever heard of the World Wide Web? The web originally stems from a U.S. Defense Department program called ARPANET (Advanced Research Projects Agency Network), established in 1969 with connections between computers at the University of California at Los Angeles, Stanford Research Institute, the University of California-Santa Barbara, and the University of Utah. ARPANET's purpose was to conduct research into computer networking in order to provide a secure and survivable communications system in case of war. As the network quickly expanded, academics and researchers in other fields began to use it as well. They saw it as a great way to have experts from different fields and locations to come together to work together provide information, solve problems and get things done.

If you look past all of the shopping, marketing and online dating ever present today, the internet still functions as a unique way for teams of people to come together to get things done.

Now, these are certainly not the fixed in stone, permanent teams organizations tend to still favor, today. These are different people coming together for only a short time to solve common issues or complete relevant tasks. Want some ideas about potential future opportunities for your business? Pull together an appropriate group of people, get them together in a room (even if it's a chat room) and watch what happens. BreakOUT city.

For example, let's say you were among senior leadership at a hospital. You wanted ideas on how to improve patient satisfaction scores. Who would you get to work on this? Nurses? Doctors? Administrators? Janitorial staff? Volunteers? Counselors? Cafeteria staff?

Now, imagine you picked your team and had them come together for the sole purpose of coming up with the three quickest and easiest ways to increase patient satisfaction by 20 percent in the next six months. What could you do with that information?

Most likely, this team of people never have sat in the same room together before much less shared ideas or developed solutions together. And, once the task has been completed, they may never have that kind of direct contact with one another again. They would all go back to their regular jobs but with a few big differences. In addition to having completed their appointed task, team members could have:

- Built a sense of community
- Increased their understanding/empathy for other concerns and work roles in areas other than their own within the organization
- Increased loyalty and interest in the organization

The best example of spontaneous, task-oriented teaming that has been used for centuries is our own jury system. Twelve people come together for the sole purpose of determining the guilt or innocence of a person accused of committing a crime. That is the total extent of their task. They are presented with the information they need, are sequestered while they deliberate and make a determination, announce their verdict and then disband – hopefully taking away a better understanding of the justice system and a sense of pride at doing their civic duty.

Within organizations, it's the same idea, just different application. Bring a unique group of people together to get a job done and then letting them get back to their regular duties. Sounds simple but many organizations have used this strategy to reach incredible levels of BreakOUT.

BreakOUT Spontaneous Task-Oriented Teams Questions

❑ Are their any issues, challenges, opportunities or tasks that I could get help with from others within my organization?

❑ How could spontaneous, task-oriented teams benefit my organization?

❑ How would teaming affect my employees and the culture of the organization?

❑ How could I implement spontaneous, task-oriented teaming in my organization?

Engagement Practices
BreakOUT H.C. Practice 14 – Leader Rounding
A practice similar to a doctor or nurse making rounds. Leaders make frequent rounds to their teams to have the opportunity to engage in two-way communication and exchange feedback.

Imagine for a moment you are a patient in a hospital. The most critical part of your day is when the doctor(s) and nurses come into your room and communicate with you. This interaction determines your attitude and the direction and flow of your day.

As a doctor or nurse, the visit lets you gauge the progress of your patient. It alerts you to the small details that point to either positive progress or possible future complications. Your presence alone brings peace of mind to your patient and reassures you, as well, that the best treatment is being offered and carried out.

As a leader, you are the "doctor" to your employees. You need to offer them the care they need to stay healthy and productive. So, just like a doctor, you need to do rounds.

Leader Rounding is exactly what it sounds like. Leaders make "rounds" to see all of their employees. They take the time to make frequent visits to their employees for the sole purpose of interacting with them.

Leader Rounding, however, is more than just walking around and just being seen (even though this does have considerable value). Rounding is a very purposeful activity – a deliberate effort to develop relationships with people so that they feel free to communicate and share their needs/ideas and for you to communicate and share yours. It needs to be planned, timed and oriented to allow a leader to have the maximum impact in line with their goals.

A first response to Leader Rounding is often "I don't have the time." You must make the time. Make rounding a priority.

Rather than "taking away" from productivity, it will add so much more productivity for you, the leader, and your team. Rounding offers an excellent opportunity for leaders to coach and mentor their teams and eliminates the most troublesome of concerns, "My leader doesn't really know what goes on around here."

BreakOUT Leader Rounding Questions

❑ Do I currently "make rounds" within my organization?

❑ How could rounding benefit my ability to lead my team?

❑ What reaction might my people have to my making rounds?

❑ What are other ways that I am visible within the organization?

BREAKOUT

Chapter 12
BreakOUT Culture Practices
(Cultivating Cultures of Choice)

The culture of your organization has the ability to catapult you to great heights or bring you to your knees. It can be one of the most powerful tools you have. This incredible social influence has the capacity to be positive, negative, effective and ineffective. Much of it is not good or bad – it simply *is*. However, one thing is certain – the stronger your organization's culture, the more cohesive and effective your team is. And the more likely your company is to survive in the organizational "jungle."

Your culture operates at the conscious and unconscious levels. It's quite simply "the way we do things around here." However, the effects are far reaching. Your culture communicates how employees speak to each other, feel about each other, dress, provide customer service, solve problems, how long a lunch "hour" really is – *everything*. Employees just *know what to do*. This influence demands that your culture not happen "by accident", but be created very deliberately and thoughtfully.

Now, there is a particular conundrum in terms of culture. It's a bit like the eternal chicken and egg debate. Is a culture determined by how people behave or do people behave in certain ways based on the culture? The answer is, yes. Sometimes people determine what the culture will be and sometimes the culture determines what people will be and do. However, as a leader, there are things you can do to affect the culture of your organization.

The following culture strategies are designed for you, as a leader, to lay an egg in terms of determining your culture. The idea being that the "message" and/or "intention" behind these strategies will be absorbed by the culture and made a part of it. In all cases, these strategies will be most effective if applied globally to the entirety of your organization. Piecemeal efforts will not get the job done here. To affect a culture, you have to be totally committed and continuously, consistently and forcefully drive the strategy through the organization.

Here are the six BreakOUT Human Capital Practices that are Culture Practices.

15. Status Neutral Culture
16. Learning & Innovation Culture
17. Flexible Flextime Culture
18. No Secrets Culture
19. No Excuses Culture
20. Celebration Culture

Culture Practices

BreakOUT H.C. Practice 15 – Status Neutral Culture

Level off excessive perks that create barriers between leaders and the people they are trying to lead.

This practice may seem simplistic but it plays a very important role in rebalancing the equity equation for employees. We are not saying that employees want their CEO to work out of the cubical next to theirs. Most employees understand that their bosses will make more money or get more stock options, or even some other perks. But, these extras need to be seen as competitively justified or tied to the business.

When the top brass proudly hang a newly purchased piece of art in the lobby purchased with corporate funds or throw a swanky party celebrating a recent merger on a yacht only days after announcing layoffs, this destroys the sense of equity in the organization. It is surprising how easily executives delude themselves into thinking they are entitled to privileges that are neither necessary to their jobs nor appropriate perks for their position. It goes way beyond obscene salaries and huge options; it's about a form of corporate elitism that chokes off employees' desire to use their discretionary effort.

Even little perks like reserved parking, corner offices, or lofty titles can seem on the surface to be acceptable corporate rewards, but these status distinctions can have a nasty consequence – they cut leaders off from the very people they are trying to lead, inhibiting open communication and interaction.

The perks that come from status distinctions may seem like "just desserts" to the people who receive them, but what they often end up doing is creating envy and resentment in those who are lower down on the corporate ladder. There is food for thought in the old adage,

> *You will never impress those who have more and*
> *you will only stir envy in those who have less.*

Inappropriate perks often lead people away from focusing on the job at hand. Internal competition sparked by the distribution of "perks" often causes people to focus on aspects of equity that are unproductive and unprofitable. Bitter thoughts like, "If she has that title, so should I!" or "I've been here longer but he got the office with a window" may result.

Reducing status distinctions and distributing "perks" equitably creates a more level playing field between leaders and their employees so that everyone can focus on the real work to be done. Taking away the "boss" and "employee" labels creates and nurtures a team-based culture where everyone is working together to contribute to the success of the organization. And where everyone's input and feedback are equally valued.

BreakOUT Status Neutral Culture Questions

❑ What kind of status distinctions exist within my organization?

❑ Do these distinctions have any repercussions in terms of how my team views the distribution of equity in the organization?

❑ How could I help "level the playing field" in terms of status distinctions in my organization?

Culture Practices

BreakOUT H.C. Practice 16 – Learning & Innovation Culture

Cultivate an environment that values, recognizes and rewards learning more, and more quickly, than the competition and leverages new and better practices throughout the organization.

Where will organizations find their sustainable competitive advantage in the future? Technology? Merger? Downsizing? Highly unlikely. Today, the true value of an organization comes from creating new knowledge that can be translated into more efficient ways of doing business. Not too surprisingly, the best resource any company has for new ideas is its own people. If companies can nurture a corporate culture that has a healthy dissatisfaction for the status quo – where every employee is committed to continuous improvement – not only will they move ahead of the competition, they'll stay there.

How does this concept fit into the Equity Equation? When learning, creativity and innovation, along with the sharing of knowledge, is valued, recognized and rewarded by the organization, all kinds of ideas will spring up – because employees know that the organization appreciates and encourages new thinking. Give people encouragement and reward for doing something you want them to do and they'll keep on doing it, and more of it. (And, by the way, this learning/creativity component is even more important to younger generations who make it part of their job criteria). One way of showing employees that this new thinking is valued is to give them the time and opportunity to develop themselves and share what they have learned.

Now, many companies say that's what they do. These are the same companies who believe that a suggestion box is sufficient to encourage input from employees. It isn't. In fact, a corporate culture where learning is genuinely welcomed hardly ever exists. The reality is that employees find that they're so caught up in getting the day-to-day tasks done that there's no time left over to learn anything new. Or, if employees do have ideas, the organizational culture frequently finds ways to sabotage their speaking out.

There's a difference between just asking for suggestions and engaging employees – between being a mouthpiece for change and actually pushing up your sleeves, opening the channels to learning and working together to make change happen. If a company wants experimentation, new ideas and practices, then it has to convince its people that if they contribute new ideas or practices that actually are put into effect, the organization will recognize and reward the people who created them.

BreakOUT Learning & Innovation Culture Questions

❑ How can I encourage employees to make suggestions on improving the organizations performance?

❑ Is "thinking outside the box" encouraged? How?

❑ Does the culture support the concept of continuous improvement?

❑ Does everyone in the organization understand the need for constant innovation?

❑ Does the organization have a "healthy dissatisfaction for the status quo?"

❑ Do you reward learning and innovation in your organization?

Culture Practices
BreakOUT H.C. Practice 17 – Flexible Flextime Culture
Open work schedules to allow for more freedom and, in turn, obtain increased productivity.

Do you like to have options? Do you like making choices… especially when it comes to your time? Most likely, so do the people on your team. Flextime allows people to select the hours they work. A common flextime option is being able to choose between working five eight-hour days or four ten-hour days. There are other variations to allow people to pick up their children from school, take care of an elderly parent, participate in a particular hobby or sport, continue their education and/or training at a local university, or just have some specific personal time for their own mental and physical health.

If planned well, flextime can be a great equity option to offer your employees. They will be highly appreciative when they are at work because they know that leadership understands that life does exist beyond cubicle walls. As we have said many times before, people who feel appreciated will be motivated to work all the more. On a flextime schedule, it has been documented many times that people are far more productive during the time they are at the office than if they were forced to work a more regular nine-to-five schedule.

Flextime does not mean there is a completely open schedule. If you left it completely open, it is possible your office would be a ghost town on Mondays and Fridays. You have to have limits… but the important thing is that you also offer options.

And, you receive many benefits from flextime as well. For example, as a leader, you can arrange the schedule such that your organization's hours can stretch well beyond the normal Monday through Friday, 9:00 AM to 5:00 PM standard giving your clients more access to your services (especially if they are in different time zones).

It can also help reduce overhead costs for those leaders who can work the schedule such that people can share equipment and resources because they work at opposite schedules.

However, by far, the major benefit of flextime is to prove beyond a doubt that you are building a strong employee-focused culture. Show your flexibility and your people will show you their appreciation.

BreakOUT Flexible Flextime Culture Questions

☐ Could I offer a more flexible schedule for my team?

☐ Are there any repercussions (positive or negative) from this type of schedule in terms of my business?

☐ What are the benefits to be gained by offering my team more freedom in determining their work schedule?

☐ Is it possible to arrange work hours that maximize individuals' high productivity zones?

Culture Practices
BreakOUT H.C. Practice 18 – No Secrets Culture
Create a culture where employees are provided with all the necessary information to perform their jobs.

B<small>REAK</small>OUT

Imagine having the responsibility of maintaining a checking account, including making deposits and withdrawals, without knowledge of the balance at all times. How would decisions regarding your spending be made? By the flip of a coin? By your mood or by how badly you wanted something?

What if you were hired to make the best tasting barbeque sauce in the world but no one would share the secret recipe with you? How would you make production decisions? How would you make marketing decisions? How successful would you be?

Many organizations operate under a strange belief – that withholding knowledge from their employees protects them from productivity loss.

Here is how it works. Leaders at the top of an organization know a major decision is coming down the line and, as if they have watched too many reruns of Secret Agent Man, they run around from closed-door meeting to closed-door meeting pretending that their employees don't have a clue what's going on.

You see, in their "for your eyes only" mindset, if employees know the truth about a merger, buyout, plant closing, change in leadership, revision to the cafeteria menu, etc., they would be so consumed in their personal reactions to the issue that their productivity levels would drop. It's the old "knowledge is power" syndrome – "What you don't know won't hurt you," and "What I know gives me an edge." Does this sound like an effective way to lead? It may sound a bit contrarian, but if everyone on a team is working toward the same goal – how is hiding important and critical information helping anyone or anything?

A culture of conspiracy breeds a high degree of distrust, especially between upper management and employees. If you made a point to hire good people, don't assume that they simply come to work and stick their heads in the sand. Chances are, the rumor mill has leaked whatever secret it is you are trying to keep and distorted it 1,000 times over. And, there is nothing like a juicy rumor to distract people from thinking about anything but their work.

As is true in any good relationship, communication is key. If you are afraid to tell your team the truth, you've got bigger problems than you know. A strong leader knows that honesty, forthrightness and a "no secrets" approach can be his or her greatest asset.

In the No Secrets Culture, leaders aren't threatened by a loss of power in the sharing of information but rather see openness and honesty as his or her responsibility to their organization and all employees. Leaders believe that the more their employees understand the business, the more likely they are to make decisions more in line with what you want – even if you aren't present. *They understand.*

A No Secrets Culture also demands something from employees. It's easier sometimes to stay in the dark and plead ignorance than actually face the sometimes bad and ugly truth. There is an aspect of accepting personal responsibility when you agree to be in an honest relationship – be it a personal or professional one. Employees must be willing to respect the information that is shared and what they do with it.

In the end, it is simply a matter of trust. People need to know what's going on to work effectively. If you don't trust them with that information, then they can't do their jobs. If you show your people that you trust them, they will trust you to guide them through crisis and opportunity alike.

BreakOUT No Secrets Culture Questions

❑ Do leaders in the organization share the disappointments and failures as well as the successes with employees?

❑ Have information silos been eliminated and opened up to all employees?

❑ What are the informal rules of the culture that shape employee behaviors?

❑ What would be the benefits of a No Secrets Culture?

❑ How would I implement this kind of culture within my organization?

Culture Practices

BreakOUT H.C. Practice 19 – No Excuses Culture

Create a culture that encourages accountability and responsibility as a way of life and doing business.

What does a No Excuses Culture mean to you? A No Excuses Culture means that if you say you are going to do something and are responsible for doing it, *you do it.* Personal accountability is key. You are expected to perform your work professionally, expertly, and in a timely manner the first time. *Everyone* in the workplace shares these expectations for behavior – no one is exempt.

As a result of these expectations and behaviors, business flows more smoothly. People know that others will keep up their end of the deal or there will be a darn good, and we mean *really darn good*, reason for not doing what you say you will do. Employees can plan their work with these expectations and very rarely be let down. Deadlines are kept. Reports are accurate. Phone calls are returned. Work is not delayed while waiting for someone else to do his or hers. *Everyone is held accountable.*

In order to sponsor this type of culture, leaders must put personal accountability center stage and actively encourage, support and reward people for getting things done right. The opposite of the coin is that leaders must provide consequences for failing to perform as expected and make those negative consequences just as strong as the positive ones. However, if done correctly (remember, feedback is immediate, specific and directly tied to performance) you probably won't have to provide negative consequences very often.

The No Excuses Culture requires responsible and strong leadership. Performance expectations must be clearly and consistently demonstrated. Incentive plans must be linked to performance. Deadlines must be communicated and tracked. Consequences must be prompt and certain and delivered by all on your leadership team, not only by some.

The No Excuses Culture is not for the faint of heart but the results are well worth the effort. You'll never want it any other way.

BreakOUT No Excuses Culture Questions

❑ Does the culture of the organization support accountability at every level?

❑ How do I hold people accountable?

❏ Do we allow excuses for people's behaviors in the organization?

❏ How does your culture "tell" employees how to fit in, how to succeed, how to contribute?

Culture Practices
BreakOUT H.C. Practice 20 – Celebration Culture
Make sure that when you win, you celebrate all the time, effort and energy your people put in to get you there.

We put this particular practice last because this is the one where most organizations fail to place enough value or emphasis. You've given your people a vision. You have aligned your organization to that vision. You have engaged your people to make that vision a reality. You have established a ***Choice*** culture that values people and inspires ultimate levels of productivity. The result: you win! You have tapped the human capital of those that work with you and begun a cycle that makes your goals a reality.

Now, it is time to celebrate!!

Many leaders only see what's coming next. They are so future-focused that they don't take the time to recognize how far they have come and what it took to get there – people. Celebrate accomplishments. Not just the big ones but the little ones as well. Let your culture reinforce all the hard work and keep people motivated to continue doing more. Throw a party, send out thank you notes, buy bagels, give a high-five… celebrate your success and those who helped create it.

Celebration is more than just a party. It is an acknowledgement of good work. It recognizes the effort a group of people gave to reach goals. It is a reward for a job well done. Celebrating also provides a sense of closure and achievement, allowing people to mentally close the door on one goal and start to look toward the next goal coming down the line.

BreakOUT Celebration Culture Questions

❏ Do we make the time to celebrate our successes?

❏ Do we celebrate incremental successes along the way?

❏ Do we tie the organization's celebrations to accomplishment of goals?

❏ What are the ways that you celebrate at the team, department and organizational level?

❏ Do employees have input into designing celebrations that are meaningful?

Epilogue
(The Biggest BreakOUT PCC Of All)

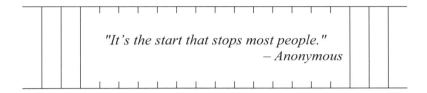

"It's the start that stops most people."
– Anonymous

This is usually the part of the book where most authors just summarize what's been said in all the previous chapters and highlight the really important stuff for you to remember. We are not going to do that. Instead, we want to leave you with a vivid image of why BreakOUT is so difficult for most of us. A story to explain, inspire and motivate.

Monkey Business

In their book, **Competing For The Future**, Gary Hamel and C.K. Prahalad describe a study done by animal behaviorists. In the study, a group of monkeys were put in a room. In the center of the room was a pole and at the top of the pole was a nice, juicy bunch of bananas. Monkeys being monkeys, they immediately started to climb the pole to get at those beautiful, bountiful, bananas. But, each time one of the monkeys would reach the top of the pole and make a grab for the bananas, they were rudely hit by a jet of cold water directed from a showerhead on the ceiling. Naturally, the monkeys screeched in outrage and jumped back away from the pole… and the prized bananas. Each monkey had to be drenched several times before they finally gave up. In the end, the monkeys were well conditioned not to go after the bananas no matter how badly they wanted one.

The study didn't end there. After a time, the animal behaviorists decided to put a new monkey in with the conditioned group. Of course, the moment the new monkey saw the bananas, he made a beeline for the pole. But, the new monkey never actually got high enough up the pole to trigger the cold shower. Why? The other monkeys – the pre-conditioned ones – yanked the new monkey back down, sometimes violently. They wouldn't let him climb the pole. After several tries, but without ever getting wet, the new monkey also gave up on getting his hands on the yummy bananas. His fellow primates prevented him from even making the climb.

The behaviorists weren't finished yet. They continued adding new monkeys one-by-one while slowly removing all of the original pre-conditioned monkeys. Finally, only new monkeys remained… ones who had never been dowsed by the cold shower. In fact, the showerhead was even removed from the room. Despite the fact that they had never actually been drenched with cold water… and the fact that there wasn't even a showerhead to blast them anymore… none of the monkeys even tried to climb the pole much less reach for the bananas. They had been conditioned that it wasn't worth the risk. You had a whole group of monkeys who prevented each other from reaching for the desired fruit and they didn't even know why they were stopping themselves.

It's a case of monkey see, monkey do. And we do it, too. Yes, we are the monkeys. They represent us. This is the perfect example of the biggest Premature Cognitive Commitment that any of us face. We have been conditioned to believe, as a group, that BreakOUT is simply not possible. Our dreams are out of reach and are literally, forbidden fruit.

For reasons we think we "know" or are blind to, we stop ourselves from reaching for what we really want out of life long before we even trying for it. When working with groups of people, we keep each other back. Can you think of anyone in your life that has given you the cold shower?

Others of us might have at some point in our lives reached for that coveted banana and got blasted by a shower that felt like it came from a fire hose. With all the pressure we have to be responsible and do the "right" things in our lives and in our businesses, we don't even try to go after our ultimate banana. We just know that we are either going to get pulled back down off the pole or get blasted if we go for the top. We've stopped trying because we have been taught not to believe anymore.

Our final message to you, dear leader, is to reject this debilitating PCC. Find it in your mind and get rid of it. Tell yourself you will believe. BreakOUT is possible. You can get what you want either as an individual, or as a leader inspiring those around you to ultimate success. You hear about people doing it all the time but, for most of you, it's not part of your experience. You think it can't happen to you. It can... and it will... if you choose.

The biggest BreakOUT you can make is to actually believe BreakOUT is possible in all areas of your personal and professional life. Take what you now know and unleash your human capital... both for yourself and for those you lead.

B<small>REAK</small>OUT

ABOUT THE AUTHORS

Richard C. Huseman, Ph.D.

Dick Huseman serves as an executive coach, keynote speaker, and consultant. He has had a variety of experiences in business school settings, serving as professor, department head, and dean. Working with companies like AT&T, Coca Cola, ExxonMobil, Florida Hospital and IBM, his focus has been in the areas of knowledge management, change management, and most importantly, relationship management.

Dick has co-authored 11 books, including his most recent works, *Give-To-Get Leadership: The Secret of the Hidden Paycheck* (2002) and *The Leader As Coach: How To Coach A Winning Team* (2004), as well as its precursor, *Managing The Equity Factor* (1989), which has been translated into Russian, German, Chinese, Portuguese, and Greek. **BreakOUT** is the culmination of over 20 years research into the organizational performance and the dynamics of human behavior in relationships.

Pamela A. Bilbrey

Pam Bilbrey is President of the Baptist Health Care Leadership Institute and shares her insights and experiences as a change leader with colleagues across the nation and internationally. As a consultant, coach and professional speaker she actively assists organizations in achieving greater levels of service and operational excellence.

Pam also continues to work closely with Baptist Health Care on its journey to excellence providing coaching and guidance in her role of Senior Vice President of Corporate Development. Her work includes a focus on driving patient, employee and physician loyalty and developing a strong leadership team for this award-winning organization.

Pam has a Masters of Science degree, a MBA degree and over twenty-four years in organizational leadership positions.